WORKING WITH PORCUPINES

Before You Begin

Please answer the following questions honestly. Don't think too much. Just check a box describing how you feel and move on.

0 = Not at all; 1 = A little; 2 = Sometimes; 3 = A lot; and 4 = Always

How do you feel as a **team member** in your current project or program?	0 Not at all	1 A little	2 Sometimes	3 A lot	4 Always
My contributions are valued by my teammates and management.					
I am very competent at the work I do on the teams to which I belong.					
Teammates seek me out for my knowledge and skill in one or more areas. I am their go-to person.					
My expertise is noticed at levels above my boss (briefings to senior people, customers, etc.)					
I am recognized in my industry for the work I do (panel memberships, published papers, etc.)					
Subtotal score is:_____					

How do you feel about the technical teams you are leading?	0 Not at all	1 A little	2 Sometimes	3 A lot	4 Always
Colleagues are eager to join the teams I lead.					
I feel very competent as a Team Leader.					
My boss and I discuss my performance at least quarterly and I am appreciated.					
I am mentoring others in the teams I am leading.					
I am growing in my skillset with at-least-annual training programs and education in the latest techniques, processes, tools, etc.					
Subtotal score is: _____					

How do you feel about the projects you manage as a project manager?	0 Not at all	1 A little	2 Sometimes	3 A lot	4 Always
My work as a Project Manager is valued by my teammates and my management.					
I feel very competent as a project manager.					
I am currently mentoring others in project management.					
My boss and I are planning my next job after this project and it involves a promotion.					
I read constantly to stay abreast of new project manager techniques and tools.					
Subtotal score is: _____					

Add the three subtotal scores to get your *grand total*: Team Member (Contributor) Score + PM Score + Team Leader Score = Total Score

What does that score indicate about your skills and overall satisfaction with your work?

Score	Meaning and Impact
0-4	You have few if any skills that are recognized by your peers or leadership. We will need to fix that.
5-8	People with these scores have only a small positive impact in their organizations. But it is a start.
9-12	This is a good start. Your influence can grow from here.
13-16	Scores in this bracket show definite potential for excellent performance on teams of all types. Building on this will boost your impact.
17-23	You are having a positive impact in several key areas of involvement. You deserve to be noticed, promoted and given some choice assignments!
24-29	Scores in this range are promising. You are seeing recognition for your skills and hard work. There is still room to improve in this realm and fine tune your skills.
30	This is outstanding!

Advance Praise for

Working with Porcupines

Mack McKinney has an engaging writing style, and this book is worth reading even if you have no plans to manage projects or lead people. Mack's career has been unusually broad and varied, and throughout the book, he drives key points home by describing pertinent real-world events he has personally experienced. It's often difficult for a reader to grasp the real meaning of pure words and definitions, but Mack's fascinating anecdotes provide a context often missing in similar works. Reading this provides a roadmap not only for successful program management but also for a fulfilling and happy life.

*— Noel Longuemare, former Principal Deputy
Undersecretary of Defense for Acquisition and Technology*

Mack's leadership and management guidance is fully developed, illustrated, and substantiated in a way that allows the reader to seamlessly apply it to a broad array of current and future challenges. Mack's 24 project management Rules are drawn from everyday life and work experiences, forged in the crucible of air combat, and ready to be applied to the most challenging individual, community, and national situations, both today and tomorrow.

*— Colonel Neil Kacena, USAF, retired. Former Dep.
Director, Lockheed Martin Skunkworks*

Mack McKinney is a uniquely gifted man who can boil down incredibly complicated concepts and issues into digestible elements that anyone can understand and then put to work. I have known him for more than a dozen years and watched him do that with everything from designing the countermeasures on modern fighter aircraft, to enticing the best out of the most complex of all things, the people around us.

*— Colonel John "JV" Venable, US Air Force, Ret.
Former Squadron Commander and Flight Lead,
USAF Thunderbirds*

Working with
PORCUPINES

24 Ways To *Sharpen* Your Leadership Style

Terry "Mack" McKinney

MERIPOINT BOOKS

Published by Meripoint Books LLC, P.O. Box 1512 Williamsburg, Virginia 23185
Cover design © by Anneliese Brei

Image credits: Permission to use the sketches has been granted by Photomania (www.photomania.net), August 2023;

Discounts for bulk purchases may be discussed with the author at mack@smoothprojects.org

Liability Disclaimer: The publisher and author have made every effort to ensure the accuracy of the information presented in this book. However, they make no representations or warranties with respect to the completeness or accuracy of the contents of this book and specifically disclaim any implied warranties of merchantability or fitness for a particular purpose. The advice and strategies contained herein may not be suitable for your situation. You should consult with a professional where appropriate. Neither the publisher nor the author shall be liable for any loss of profit or any other commercial damages, including but not limited to special, incidental, consequential, or other damages. Readers should be aware that Internet websites offered as citations and/or sources for further information may have changed or disappeared between the time this was written and when it's read.

Portions of this book are memoirs and are based on the author's present recollections about events that occurred years ago, and his opinions about those events, so there may be inaccuracies and errors of omission and commission. Examples and case studies use information from third party sources and have been changed to remove direct associations with any person(s), living or deceased. Names and locations have been changed to protect the privacy and identities of the individuals and organizations involved and to avoid embarrassing, libeling or offending any person or organization. This book is not intended as a substitute for professional medical advice and is not meant to be used, nor should it be used, to diagnose or treat any medical or psychological condition. Readers are advised to consult their own medical advisors regarding mental or other health issues.

The appearance of U.S. Department of Defense (DoD) visual information does not imply or constitute DoD endorsement. The use of corporate names or logos is not meant to allege or imply endorsement. The use of military organization or unit names, symbols or insignia is not meant to allege or imply endorsement. The quoting of other sources, authors and documents is not meant to allege or imply endorsement.

Paperback ISBN 9781735611891
Printed in the United States of America.
First Edition.

MERIPOINT BOOKS

Text: Book Antiqua 10 pt

This book is dedicated to the next generations of leaders. I hope the rules, lessons learned, and stories ease your path as you tackle new projects and programs, develop systems, manage yourself and lead others.

Remember that your life, itself, qualifies as a project as we define it in these pages—an organized effort (well, sometimes), with a beginning (your birth) and end (your death), designed to fulfill your unique mission. You get to design your life-project while you live it. We hope these 24 *Rules* will help you do that.

Preface

Porcupines are odd creatures. They are rodents, usually solitary and anti-social, near-sighted and slow moving. They destroy trees and anything leather. So, metaphorically speaking, you do not want to be a solitary, unapproachable, antisocial, rodent-like person who never builds and only destroys, and who others avoid as much as possible, do you? The danger is that, like porcupines who surely do not see their behavior as abnormal (at least for porcupines), you may already be unknowingly exhibiting porcupine-like behavior! How would you know?

Curious dogs, wolves and other predators sniff unsuspectingly around porcupines only to get whacked with a tail armed with tiny spears that cause excruciating pain. Left untreated, animals that have been thwacked in the face can die of starvation because they cannot eat.

Carrying this analogy a little further, we find that the porcupine's best-known trait, its roughly 30,000 quills, have parallels in life and business. Those tiny weapons can cause major problems for people.

Life presents us with unseen dangers and challenges. Difficult people and complex projects can be porcupine-like: easy to manage until you are working close to them, then WHACK! You find major, unforeseen problems.

While we must deal with these porcupines in life and work, we do not have to be injured by them—we can, instead, avoid them, outmaneuver them and minimize the adverse impacts they might have. The 24 Rules in this book are designed to help team leaders do exactly that.

You Can Smooth-Out the Bumps in Your Life

This book will help you in at least three ways. First, by giving you easily understood rules, techniques and hacks you can use immediately to make your life and your projects go smoothly. Second, by showing you the key lessons I have learned and benefitted from, with examples to make you a resounding success at anything you try. And finally by preventing you from making the inadvertent mistakes other people have made that derailed their professional lives and complicated their personal lives unnecessarily. Each rule has some mix of these three benefits for you and many feature all three.

The rules presented in this book are universal and apply to anything management or leadership-related. They can be used for all projects and activities. They can make you successful on projects ranging from selecting a neighborhood for a family move, to leading a sales team in the hospitality industry. You can use them to design a new motorcycle, to build a new wide area network for an office complex, or to architect a new way to detect hard-to-find missile threats in a combat environment (literally — I have done just that a few times, using these rules).

Applying these rules can mean the difference between projects that succeed versus those that fail, team members who work well together versus those who fight constantly, or a career that launches like a rocket versus one that flames out on the launchpad.

Many of the examples in this book are from the world of defense systems, because that is where my experience lies. The rules themselves are much more widely applicable.

For most rules, we have provided examples, many of which have been sanitized to disguise the usually-guilty companies and/or individuals involved.

You Can Control the Older Generations

In this book you will learn how older generations think, what motivates them — basically how to influence them and when you get it all exactly right, how to control them. Yep, I am giving you the inside track on how our brains work, something no geezer in their right mind should disclose to younger generations. I am doing this for a serious reason — it's best for our culture and our society. All four generations in the workforce at any one time must work together, not separately, to solve society's ills and make a better place for our children and grandchildren.

PhotoMania

The Event that Pushed Me Over the Edge

Have you ever tried to open a hotel room door where everything works as designed, the little green light illuminates, but the #%@&?!! handle just will not open the door latch? While you are tired and soaking wet? At 1 AM? Well, I have.

What Happened?

After a long day and flight from Baltimore, Maryland to Fort Worth, Texas to teach a systems engineering class at the Lockheed Martin Skunk Works, I sprinted in driving rain from the car to the hotel. The desk clerk gave me my electronic key card, and I squeaked down the hall in my squishy wet shoes to my room which, of course, was at the far end of the hall.

I inserted the card into the slot, withdrew it and promptly got a green light. YEAH! With a sigh of relief, knowing I was finally going to be able to get out of those wet clothes and get some sleep, I pressed the door handle downward and ... nothing. The door was still tightly latched and the lovely, welcoming green light — went — out. The handle had turned but the latch remained closed, and the door would not open. Three more attempts yielded the same result: a widening pool of water around my feet from my dripping coat, my blood pressure increasing by the second, and a tightly latched frigging door.

Appointing myself an honorary mechanical engineer, I concluded that it had to be a failed internal latch mechanism. Dejected, I dropped my bags in the hallway and slogged back to the front desk. The desk clerk wanted to make me a new key but I assured him that my key worked in the lock (green light, remember) so the electronic part of this entire system appeared to be working. I asked him to get someone to change out the lock and he said they did not have a maintenance person on-site at 1 AM. I asked him for another room. He sheepishly informed me that the hotel was full, and he had no other rooms to give me.

My military mindset took over for a moment and I mentally cycled through all the ways I would get into that room including, since it was the ground floor, prying open and climbing into the window! No kidding—I had done that before and I was ready to try anything now! But just for grins, I asked him to accompany me down to the room and see if he could get that door to open. Honestly, I planned to get him to take a screwdriver or something and pry that door latch open so I could get into that room, and since it would be a hotel employee who did the damage to the door, I would not be charged for the damage. That was my devious plan.

He took my key card, got the green light, turned the handle and the door popped open! Being the backyard scientist that I am, I said "give me that key!" I slid the key in and out, got the green light, pushed the handle down and ... nothing. The door stayed latched. What kind of hotel sorcery was this? This just would not register in my exhausted brain! So I asked him to open it again and this time I watched carefully—he was turning the door handle UPWARD.

Coming to my senses, I stopped the experiment, just in case the latch might actually fail, and I WOULD be stranded in that hallway. I asked him if all the doors in the hotel functioned that bass-ackward way, where the handle moved upward instead of downward, and he said quite a few of the doors were that way. He said, when the electronic door latch system was updated throughout the hotel, the installer had apologized that he had accidentally installed some door "pins" incorrectly and those doors would require the handle to be turned upward, not downward, to function. It was a simple choice of pin direction (vertical or horizontal) and he had not paid much attention to direction when installing the latches. Nobody made him correct those other doors. More on this stroke-inducing situation later in the book.

This phenomenon is not limited to that hotel! Look at this door in a prestigious US East Coast hospital!

Flawed system designs (and good designs but bad *installations*) abound! And they must be stopped.

If your life is not driven by Rules, it will likely be driven by crises.

Mistakes Have Power

I have learned a lot from the teams I have led and the projects I worked on through the years, from the mistakes I saw and, in many cases, caused or at least participated in. This collection of mistakes and the rules that can prevent them has grown to hundreds of examples. This book features the most important of these rules and lessons, selected specifically for you. The few defense-related examples cited here will give people without military experience a glimpse into the difficult yet rewarding lives and missions of our amazing US and Allied warfighters and the technical professionals who support them.

I wrote this book because the eager, energized professionals who are coming behind my generation need to know the key reasons for the difficulties they may have as they try to assimilate into a professional workforce, and how to fix them. They face unique challenges:

- Four generations of people are working concurrently and the oldest and the youngest generations see the world very differently. Most of a new employee's managers will be older. Unlike college, young employees now find themselves in the age-minority at work. This itself is a critical concern since it illustrates the difficulty that defense firms are having in recruiting and retaining new professionals.

- When senior employees entered the workforce years ago, the corporate environment was different than today. Consider salaries for example: If you shared your salary number with someone else, and management found out, you were likely to be fired. Now, websites specialize in keeping track of what each position pays at each firm. New employees in many companies routinely discuss salary and benefits. Many senior people, me included, still find this openness about compensation unsettling.

- If you cannot wrap your brain around the nuances of working with different generations, start thinking of them as being from an entirely different culture and geographic area on the planet. For example, if you are a young Black professional raised in New York City, and your new boss is a much older Caucasian Baby Boomer from timber-cutting country in Oregon, there are likely to be differences in your worldviews. Read books on how each generation is "wired." Here are some terrific books on Generational and Digitally Induced Behaviors:

  - Nicholas Carr, "The Shallows" (London: Atlantic Books, 2010)

  - Lynne C. Lancaster and David Stillman, "When Generations Collide" (New York: HarperCollins, 2005)

  - Mark Bauerlein, "The Dumbest Generation" (New York: Penguin Group, 2009)

  - Mack R. Hicks, PhD, "The Digital Pandemic" (Far Hills, NJ: USA, New Horizons Press, 2010)

  - Johann Hari, "Stolen Focus" (New York: Random House, 2022)

I know something about you—without having met you! You are already doing project-related work and may even be a project leader!

You Are Your Own Project

Your first-grader's effort to build a volcano with Jell-O and dry ice is a project. Many of the things you do every day are projects, such as purchasing a car, searching for a new job, buying a Wi-Fi router, or replacing a cell phone. Without consciously thinking about it, each of these projects requires research, analysis, resource procurement, planning, and execution.

What is a "project" anyway? Definitions abound, many of them too restrictive, others too loose. One of the leading project management organizations in the industry, The Project Management Institute (PMI), describes projects[1] as having a beginning, an end, a team, a budget, a schedule and expectations. If we add *result*, we get the following definition:

> *A Project is an organized effort, with a beginning and end, designed to create a unique service, product, capability, or other result.*

With this definition in mind, let us consider a dinner that we are preparing to enjoy with friends next Saturday night. The preparation will require initial actions well known to project managers:

1. **Plan**: Number of guests, start time, dinner theme — Thai food tonight?
2. **Research**: Evaluate recipes with respect to guests' preferences and theme.
3. **Gather resources**: Find and buy ingredients.
4. **Experiment**: Whip up the sauce the recipe calls for and sample it the day prior to the dinner, be sure it's tasty but not volcano-spicy!
5. **Build a schedule**: The night before, chill wine/beer; two hours before, chop veggies; 1 hour before, set table.
6. **Execute the plan**: Prepare the food, host that meal and enjoy. *Bon Appetit!*
7. **Close out**: Clean up and put away dishes, ingredients not used, adjust recipes as needed (too spicy, etc.). The project management business calls this an After-Action Report (AAR).

As you see, you are already doing it! You are a Project Manager. Even if you do not work professionally as a project manager, in many aspects of your life, you are already managing successful projects.

Back to the Saturday evening Thai dinner: If you asked one of the invited guests to bring the rice because they have a great rice cooker, you are now *leading a team by directing the actions of other people*. If you asked another invitee to provide the rice-cooker-person with a recipe for Jasmin rice with

---

[1] In this book we use the terms *Project* and *Program* interchangeably, however, a Program is often a government-funded (contracted) project or collection of projects. A Program can also be a Program of Record (a formal designation within the US Government). All the key activities and actions necessary for successful projects also apply to Programs. The reverse is not true. All the special rules and regulations required for federal programs add several layers of additional requirements, reports, resource tracking, accounting, reviews, etc. to any project.

peas and cilantro, then you are *leading a collaborative team*: the three of you are working together toward a common goal and you are leading that effort.

Welcome to Project Management and Team Leadership! This book will show you how to become even more effective at this by giving you a framework of rules to help you make leadership decisions.

Why Bother With This Leadership Stuff Anyway?

Consider this online public post: [2]

> I have been in a lead role for multiple companies over the last 10 years, and in that time, I have gotten zero leadership training or even a walk thru of what they want it to look like. I have been trained on lean/5S and efficiencies, but never actual leadership. I wonder when companies will find that this is important enough to start spending money on it and that it really does matter.

Or this from a 33-year-old software engineer and principal investigator (PI) at a US national laboratory:

> I am leading a team of four people on a cutting-edge research project. I am in this position entirely because of my technical skills; I have no managerial experience. As a PI I'm not expected to, and nobody is offering me leadership or managerial training, even though it would be very helpful. So I'm just winging it. (name and employer redacted)

This lack of leadership training in corporate America is nothing new. Peter Drucker commented on this years ago (again, the emphasis is mine):

> Companies today aren't managing their employees' careers; knowledge workers must, effectively, be their own chief executive officers . . . It's up to you to carve out your place, to know when to change course, and to **keep yourself engaged and productive** during a work life that may span some 50 years. To do those things well, you'll need to cultivate a deep understanding of yourself— not only what your strengths and weaknesses are but also how you learn, how you work with others, what your values are, and

---

[2] LinkedIn, 2021

where you can make the greatest contribution. Because only when
*you **operate from strengths** can you achieve true excellence.* [3]

By following the *Rules* in this book and managing my own career, I'm living proof that Drucker is correct. You must make your own way, and nobody gets it perfectly "right." I certainly did not. We're each "a work in progress," right?

Rules Help Prevent Failures

Poor designs and flailing projects, usually done without guiding rules, typically fail to field. If substandard systems and devices somehow do get manufactured, fielded, and installed, they are at best frustrating to the users and may, at worst, get people killed. You can make a difference if you do two crucially important things:

1. Develop rules so you can be the leader you want to be led by. People want to work with authentic, engaged project managers and team leaders because of their confidence and expertise. An important part of confidence is a keen sense of right and wrong and—an internal set of rules for behaving ethically, managing projects, leading teams and living life.

2. As a Project Manager or Team Leader, you can help prevent poorly-designed products from ever entering service. Have you experienced poor designs in your life (like the aforementioned hotel room and bathroom door handles)? If so, you probably muttered "what idiot designed it this way?"

We have all encountered websites that are architected in a bizarre fashion and won't let you return to a previous page or won't let you see the passwords you just typed in. My wife's favorite pet-peeve is a webpage that requires a calendar date for your birthday, but instead of letting you enter it using a simple, generally accepted format such as Day/Month/Year as XX/XX/XXXX, you must click on a tiny calendar, one month at a time, all the way back to her birth year! (Yes, that is a *LOOOONG* way back.) It's all about the underlying rules with which you lead the design team.

---

[3] Managing Oneself," Peter F. Drucker, Best of HBR 1999, Harvard Business Review, January 2005, customerservice@harvardbusiness.org

Managing Projects versus *Leading* People

For many decades, the project management community has focused on **the big three**: **people**, **processes** and **tools**. The problem is that project management and leadership educators, while diving deeply into the latter two, short-change the former, the people.

Learning people-skills is difficult and few technical people enjoy it. It's messy "soft skills" stuff, and few technically minded people want to bother with it, but it's so critical to being a good leader. Traditional project management diploma mills talk about "managing" people. This is the wrong perspective. You can manage a project or program and you must manage yourself, but you will *lead* people. To do so, you must have a firm understanding of the values and rules you live by.

You already use internalized rules, possibly unrecognized and almost certainly unwritten, that guide your personal behavior. I encourage you, before reading any further, to write down your worldview. Answer the following questions: *What do I value in life? Where did I get these values? How should people be treated? What behaviors do I feel are clearly right? What do I feel is clearly wrong? What are the consequences of doing a good thing? What are the consequences of doing a bad thing?*

If you start with your firmly held convictions and then add the rules in this book that speak to you, you will create a baseline set of rules for yourself. These will become the foundational guardrails that guide your decision-making.

Chapter 1

A Framework of Essential Rules & How to Use Them

A rule is a fundamental pillar of how you think, formally defined as:

An accepted principle or instruction that states the way things are or should be done, and tells you what you are allowed or are not allowed to do.[4]

Think of a rule as something important that you think about before and during an action. Some people use rules as "checklists" of important things, employed to prevent them from forgetting something key to success. Unlike process zealots who insist that some things must never be done (Rules of Omission), while everything else must always be done a certain way (Rules of Commission), I believe systems design, project management and team leadership activities, including launching a new business, are "best effort" actions, to use a contracting term. Personally, we do our best to adhere to the key rules in this book, knowing that we may need to make exceptions. Humans are involved, so our decisions about anything will seldom be cut-and-dried. Let most of these rules firmly guide your actions, not dictate or prohibit them.

Be forewarned: whenever you violate your own rules, it will bother you. It will not feel right, and you're likely to regret it, often for a long time, and sometimes for the rest of your life. That is why it's so important to get your rules down on paper and use them to guide your everyday actions. I talk about personally wrestling with this weakness later in the book.

So, here is a framework that gives you the tools to work well with other people, lead projects and reduce surprise by other people's actions. This framework is a jumpstart on developing your own collection of rules, with examples of things you should always try to do; ways in which you should always behave; and never behave. We include real-world lessons learned and illustrative examples.

---

[4] Cambridge Dictionary Online https://dictionary.cambridge.org/us/dictionary/english/rule

How to Use This Book

After 50 years of trial and error and with the hope of staying true to my personal values, I have synthesized 144 time-tested rules for leading people and managing projects. No worries, only the 24 most essential ones are presented to you in the chapters that follow. These rules are sometimes intertwined and/or combined, but I have untangled them for you. We start with 24 Essential Team Leadership Rules. The next book in the series will provide Essential Project Management Rules, plus Essential Ethics Rules. Our use of the term *Rules* is first-letter capitalized to distinguish it from more general uses of the term "rule."

Decades ago, I enjoyed reading the book *A Pattern Language*.[5] I've used the basic layout of the "Patterns" in this book: each *Rule* begins with an *observation* regarding the challenge we are addressing. This is followed by *discussion* and *examples* to illustrate key points and to provide context. After the discussion, we offer one or more *calls-to-action* in bold type.

Now, I present to you the 24 Team Leadership Rules for Leading a Team Without Losing Your Mind.

---

[5] Christopher Alexander et al, A Pattern Language (New York: Oxford University Press, 1977)

24 Useful Rules

Chapter 2

Successful Team Selection and Planning

Rule 1: Frame First or Fail

Rule 2: Set the Vision

Rule 3: Speak Up or Do Without

Rule 4: Check the Mirror

Rule 1. Frame First or Fail

> Observation: People cannot effectively address a problem until everyone on the team agrees on what the actual problem is.

When first discussing a need, people often neglect to clearly define the problem in a way that is acceptable and understandable to all major players. But if you do not agree on the exact problem to be solved, what can you expect, except perhaps a disaster down the road?

Savvy Project Team Leaders use some sort of simple technique to communicate what they want. There are many methods available. One that is widely used in the project management community is the problem-framing method pioneered by Dr. Edward Crawley,[6] which requires the completion of the following statements:

> **We want to**… (enterprise or stakeholders' intent, or the "why" you are attacking the problem; what value are you trying to create?)
>
> **By**… (the "how," using solution-neutral verbs such as create, destroy, transport, transform, compare, etc.)
>
> **Using**… (the "what," or statement of structure; this introduces cost)
>
> **While**… (detailing other important goals or constraints).

Example 1: You need a dentist in the town where your family will be moving. The wrong way to find one is to sign up with the dentist featured on the promotional flyer that was left in your mailbox. Instead, the right way to find one is to do a proper framing of the problem. It might look like this:

> **We want to** find a dentist who has a good reputation for quality work at reasonable prices, located within a 20-minute drive from both work and home.

---

[6] Professor of Aeronautics and Astronautics and of Engineering Systems, MIT. https://aeroastro.mit.edu/research-areas/systems-design-engineering

By researching dentists in various locations and specialties, in group and solo practice.

Using recommendations from friends and colleagues, our insurance company, and Health Grades™

While remembering that one of our children has a serious fear of dentists and will need special handling and meds, and one adult in our family needs a porcelain crown, so acceptance of our dental insurance will be key.

Example 2. Starting a small business to help pay college bills. I was a first-year student at the University of Kentucky. I lived near campus and rode a bicycle to class. I wanted to move into an apartment with two friends and the only apartment we could afford was a 20 minute drive from campus. I worked in the Student Cafeteria but could never seem to save much money. My parents were helping me financially as much as they could, and we had always planned for me to get a better job after my first year. FEDEX in Lexington offered flexible hours so I interviewed. They then did me a huge favor—by not hiring me. I was too scrawny and they thought I would not be able to handle heavy packages for a four-hour shift. Had they hired me, I probably would never have started my own business at college.

During the summer between my first and sophomore years, I worked on a highway construction crew and saved enough money to buy a 10-year-old Austin Healey 3000 from my uncle, but I was unable to save any additional money for my share of rent, fuel, groceries, etc. in the upcoming year. I was STUCK! This is what my project framing would have looked like:

I wanted to generate income when I started the sophomore semester.

By entering a flexible business where I could schedule my own hours, around my classes, and not have to work so many hours that it impacted my grades.

Using my existing knowledge and skills, or those I could learn quickly, because I only had three months to prepare before my sophomore year started.

Without spending a lot of money and time setting up a business (because I didn't have the money or the time).

My mother owned and managed a music store and my dad had taught himself to tune pianos there. Dad encouraged me to research what piano tuners earned, so I did and learned they made in one hour what most people earned in five hours of work! That summer, dad taught me to tune pianos and I practiced, under his watchful eye, at the music store mom operated.

That fall when I began the next semester, I visited the main music store in Lexington, Kentucky, and offered my services as a tuner. The owner wanted to see me demonstrate my skills so I brought my tools, which dad had graciously donated to my cause, and tuned the first of many pianos for that business.

Every business needs reliable, predictable cash flow. Tuning pianos for the music store provided good income but it was sporadic business, driven by deliveries of new pianos from the factories to the music store, every 4-6 weeks. I needed to find additional piano tuning jobs. Since weekends were class-free, I researched tuning pianos in the surrounding communities. Like any business, I needed to advertise to potential customers. I reasoned that at least some people with pianos would be taking lessons from piano teachers in their communities. These were the days before the Internet so I looked up piano teachers in the Yellow Pages of communities within a 90-minute drive of Lexington, Kentucky. I offered to tune their pianos for free if they would arrange four piano tunings with their students. To my pleasant surprise, most of these teachers welcomed me with open arms — they complained that getting a piano tuner to drive out from Lexington had always been a major problem and that many of their students' pianos were badly out of tune. So I spent many weekends tuning pianos in the surrounding communities.

My girlfriend Cindy's family included an aunt in London, Kentucky. She was a music teacher and I worked the same arrangement with her, tuning her piano for free if she pre-sold four other piano tuning gigs for me on a weekend.

This turned out to be an excellent business and paid for a car, fuel, my share of apartment rent, meals and books.

This framing technique is simple and helpful in clarifying what you, as the team leader, and all stakeholders will be striving to achieve.

Therefore:

> ➤ **Frame every problem before doing anything else on a project, program or task. Keep working on the framing until all key team members agree fully.**

> ➤ **Use a recognized framing approach such as that developed by Dr. Crawley.**

➤ Start your own business! To enhance your chances of succeeding, do your homework.

➤ Get a kick-start from someone already in that business (my dad tuned pianos and taught me how).

➤ Do what others are not willing to do (understandably, tuners were unwilling to drive 90 minutes to tune one piano, so I arranged to tune many).

➤ Look for underserved customer populations (I found frustrated music teachers in outlying areas and made them my business "partners" so they could get free tunings).

Rule 2.   Set the Vision

Observation: A group of people cannot function as an effective team until they agree on their purpose in coming together.

Working together toward common goals is essential, but having a mutual understanding of the goals is often taken for granted. If a team leader does not provide a common vision, each team member will develop their own, independently. This is human nature.

In the design process, this common vision can be expressed by clearly summarizing basic requirements using a framing technique as in Rule 1 and by developing a high level conceptual view of the effort by creating what is known as a Single Page Operations Concept (SPOC).

The SPOC asks four basic questions that take the *framed problem* in Rule 1 a step further. This will provide all players—developers, users, stakeholders, sub-contractors, and finance specialists—a basic agreement on the what, why, how and where. Here is the SPOC outline:

1. **What are we trying to do?** If you do not get this right, nothing else will be right: deliverables will be wrong; team members will squabble; end users will be unhappy; and someone usually gets fired.

2. **Why are we making these changes?** In other words, what is wrong with what we have? Why bother?

3. **How will it work when it's finished?** When it's operational, how will it function, what will it do that is new?

4. **Where will the new capability fit in the real world?** No system or team operates in a vacuum. We live in systems-of-systems.

When you can answer these four fundamental questions on one side of a sheet of paper, then you might know enough to get started.

Example. Companies in the defense industry experience periodic downturns in revenue. During one such downturn, the company I was working for at the time imposed a major salary reduction on all employees. The chairman of the board told me that my salary would be reduced by 50%. I informed him I wanted to stay but would have to leave the company because I could not pay my family's bills with a 50% reduction in pay. We negotiated a 30% reduction in pay and an agreement that I could start a non-interfering, noncompetitive consulting business to make up for the difference in monthly income. My wife Cindy and I researched available, memorable corporate names and Solid Thinking Company was born!

The SPOC would have looked like this:

1. **What are we trying to do?** We needed to generate enough cash to make up for the 30% salary loss.

2. **Why were we making these changes?** We had an immediate cash flow problem plus we knew these dips in income could happen at any time in the future. We needed another income stream.

3. **How would it work when finished?** Ideally when one income stream was down the other one would be up. And they would be independent of each other so even if one dwindled to nothing we would still have the other.

4. **Where would the new capability fit in the real world?** I was confident I could do both jobs: my salaried business development position and my part time job as a business co-owner.

With Solid Thinking Company, as I had done in the piano tuning business, I found a niche. Defense contractors and defense organizations were being required to write *concepts of operations* or CONOPS. The market was fragmented and there were dozens of competing templates for CONOPS. I had already taught a few courses on this subject, privately, so my wife Cindy and I decided to explore CONOPS training courses as a business venture for our new company.

I wrote articles about the crucial importance of CONOPS and we launched a website. Within a year, our new business generated enough income that I left my old company and we moved closer to Washington, DC, where most of our CONOPS customers were located. We networked, wrote articles and distributed business cards at defense industry functions. It worked! At one point, seven of the top 10 Google search results directed people to our website! We operated this business for 10 years.

Therefore:

- ➤ Secure an agreement among all major project participants, using a tool such as the SPOC. Do this early in every system development, business launch or other complex effort. Do this immediately after the Problem Framing in *Rule 1*.

- ➤ Socialize the SPOC and the framed problem until there is full consensus among the stakeholders regarding the job being tackled.

- ➤ Use the SPOC and Framed Problem to form the basis of a Project Charter which should be agreed upon by you and your leadership prior to launch. When launching a business, these two tools (SPOC and Framed Problem) form the start of your business planning.

Rule 3.   Speak Up or Do Without

> Observation: Taking the time to determine the resources needed for any project or task is some of the best time any manager can spend. Actually securing those resources is even more important.

Along with Problem Framing and building a SPOC, it's important to prepare an itemized task-breakdown with associated timelines and resources needed. These are the pre-launch activities that bring the team together for brainstorming sessions and add meat to the program framework. All successful projects begin with a thorough gathering of this information. Remember, schedule and resources are critical!

If the information is not available, consider taking on that task yourself. Go get it — you will learn a lot.

While knowing what resources you will need for a project is important, equally important is getting those resources released to you and your team.

Example 1. How NOT to do it! This was one of the most important projects in my professional life, and I almost terminated it on day one. As a 1st Lieutenant in the US Air Force working in Virginia, I naively agreed to teach USAF Air Weapons Controllers (combat radar controllers) at a new school being established in West Germany. It seemed reasonable enough — I would be an instructor teaching the same material I was currently teaching. But the beer would be better. My new bride and I packed up, we said goodbye to our parents, siblings and friends, and headed to West Germany.

When I arrived in Germany and began resource planning by inspecting the school resources, I was shocked by what I did **not** have:

- **People**: There were few controllers who had heard of either Air Combat Training or Dissimilar Air Combat Training (ACT/DACT) and fewer still who were interested in learning about it. Capt. John Fite was the only person in the squadron who showed interest. He turned out to be a kindred spirit and an excellent ACT/ DACT Instructor-Controller.

- **Training** Airspace: My inspection of the available airspace for 3-dimensional F-15 Eagle air combat training was eye-popping. There was none. And commercial airliners were flying everywhere, an extreme hazard to flight safety!

- **Classrooms**: There were none. The operations building was a leaky, tar-paper-roofed shack left over from Korean War days. There were no other spaces available for classroom training.

- **Money**: There was none. I had no budget for training materials and the facility had no classified information regarding the latest Warsaw Pact (read "Russian") threat.

- **Proper Equipment**: The computer-automated radar displays were the wrong equipment for teaching controllers to visualize air combat maneuvers by high-speed F-15 fighter aircraft. We would be doing our DACT control in spite of our radar displays.

- **Time**: I would have no relief from my other normal squadron duties. I was still an Air Weapons Controller and a Weapons Assignment Officer in an automated Command and Control (C2) facility. My wartime duties for NATO included assigning combat air patrols and intercepts to American F-4 and F-15 fighters and ordering the interception of hostile fighters using US Army Hawk surface-to-air missiles (SAMs). I also had to maintain proficiency with the C2 software. Plus I was the squadron Security Officer, leading a team of fifteen enlisted airmen armed with M-16 rifles, who defended our people and equipment when deployed for exercises or wartime operations. Each of those jobs took time.

Everyone involved with this project knew that at least some resources would be needed, but except for getting me sent to Germany, nobody had done anything to pull those resources together. When it dawned on me that I would have to personally gather the resources, find and lead the other instructors, arrange and oversee setting up the school from soup-to-nuts, including getting German airspace released to the US Air Force, and building a training program and lessons, I was flabbergasted. I would be doing all that from start to finish as a lowly Lieutenant without help from my squadron or their immediate headquarters.

I was STUCK! I had agreed to make this happen!

I told Cindy, my young bride, that I had signed up to do something that was not going to be humanly possible. I told her I should have thoroughly researched the situation from the security of my comfortable job in Virginia, before uprooting us from friends and elderly parents and moving to Europe.

I would ask to be reassigned to another unit, or at least be relieved of the school-start-up duty.

Then, a strange thing happened. While I was controlling a routine intercept training mission, I heard on my military UHF radio the familiar voices of Rocket, Hands, Kodak and Smash—F-15 pilots with whom I had worked and flown back in Virginia, and who, like me, were now assigned to a unit in Germany. They trusted all the military fighter controllers, like me, in Germany to keep them safe in the air. But these pilots, my friends, would not be able to train for the real thing for air combat in Germany without proper airspace away from civilian airliners. If war broke out, as it could at any time, they would not be ready for it, and without an air combat school for controllers my radar colleagues would not be trained to keep those pilots alive in the aerial dogfights of real combat.

That would be unacceptable. I decided to make it happen.

I "burned the boat on the beach" as the Viking captains did hundreds of years earlier to get complete commitment from the crews in staying and settling a new land. I would get that airspace opened up for the F-15 Eagle pilots and I would launch that school! I found three kindred spirits and leaned on them to help me, fellow controller Capt. John Fite, my unit commander Lt Col Al Shearer (601st Tactical Control Squadron/CC) and Col. Jim Emory at HQ US Air Forces Europe (USAFE).

Three months later we got that airspace opened up to American fighter pilots by the German government! And 45 days after that, we launched the first air combat tactics training school for fighter controllers in Europe!

Therefore:

> ➤ **Do your homework before you agree to take on a new task. Find out what resources are available to support the task before you say yes.**

> ➤ **Apply *Rules 1 & 2* to ensure everyone involved in a project is in full agreement on the scope and extent of the challenge.**

> ➤ **Follow-through with task assignments/agreements if you are a team leader and people are counting on you to succeed.**

Rule 4. Check the Mirror!

> Observation: Some people perform consistently well, give others credit, work well with diverse people, and accept crappy jobs. These habits help people move up in organizations.

Those who get noticed by leadership are humble yet effective. They don't seek the spotlight for themselves; the spotlight finds them. They work well with and respect those of different generations and backgrounds. People want to work with them.

> *Check the mirror: are you an arrogant, smirky, know-it-all who thinks it's beneath you to do insignificant tasks that are asked of you? Or are you someone who recognizes the value of doing everything, even menial tasks, with a good attitude?*
>
> —*Colonel Bill Brei, USAF, Ret.*

We all know the extremely arrogant project manager or technical team leader who dominates conversations, belittles others behind their backs, and always seeks the limelight. They are one type of prickly people and we have tips throughout this book for dealing with them. Just guard against yourself becoming arrogant or domineering: If you sense that people are not connecting with you, perhaps not respecting you or what you are saying, ask "What is wrong with me" rather than "What is wrong with them?" Look in the mirror!

What motivates the good leaders in any industry? Let's frame their challenges using Dr. Crawley's Problem Framing Technique. The good manager:

Wants to complete projects on-time and on-budget, so they contribute the agreed-upon margin to their seniors and get promoted.

By customizing their management approach to each person's unique needs, so they stay on the job and remain productive, while maintaining a reasonable work-life balance.

Using the staff, equipment and tools assigned to them.

Without burning people out with the typical stress, interpersonal conflicts that arise, and constant avalanche of administrivia from higher-ups.

So, bear these challenges in mind when you bump into personalities different from your own. We talk about how to work with and around difficult, even "prickly" people at several places in this book.

Example 1. I had a prickly situation arise when working at Westinghouse Defense. I was the new manager of an applied R&D team of eight people who were all younger than me except for one retired US Navy Captain. Raymond E. Helms Jr. was my father's age and I was worried.

Ray was the most senior member of my new staff, by decades, and we were of different generations. Worse yet, he had been passed over for the job and promotion I was given! He also was former Navy and I was former Air Force (yes, there can be serious differences). Ray was operational Navy-focused while I was technology-focused. We were not much alike and I feared he would be "prickly" to deal with. It was my first real management job at Westinghouse. It involved a tricky USD $5M license agreement with a UK firm, my boss's boss was worried about the job, and our Defense Center leadership would be watching everything. Oh yes, we also had US DOD contracts underway and they were high-visibility and high-risk.

We were ballistic testing a new piece of armor material our research team had developed. The test involved a single shot with a 9mm pistol, at a range of 40 feet. It was a "soft" armor and I believed the 9mm round would either rip it apart or bury itself in the material—either way, there was no risk to the shooter (me) or the observers (Ray and the Firing Range Supervisor). My first hint that my analysis of the threat of a ricochet might be wrong was the Range Officer, also much older than I, saying "I'll be waiting inside the office, behind some bullet-resistant glass." He left. Ray and I snickered at each other, and I may or may not have whispered "sissy."

I pressed the trigger.

BANG!

The round slammed into the target at about 800 miles per hour. Ray was standing directly behind me, on my right, and as I removed my hearing protectors he said calmly, "Mack, I think you have shot me." Just his regular, measured voice. No excitement.

I looked over and he was staring at his feet. The toe of his right shoe—hard, black leather—was dented by about an inch and a deformed bullet was rocking back and forth on the concrete floor a few inches away. Ray was right. I had shot him.

His shoe was ruined, but he was unhurt. I apologized and Ray said, "Nobody made me stand there, Mack. I thought it was safe too." The Range Officer came out of his little glass cabin, looked at the bullet and Ray's ruined dress shoe and belly-laughed at us.

After the lunch I bought Ray as penance for my ignorance, I never had doubts about getting along with him. He was cool even after being shot! I had not over-reacted to his "you shot me" words, and Ray told me later that my matter of fact "Well, are you hurt?" question told him I was a low-drama person as well.

Ray and I worked closely together for the next three years, climbing around on huge warships and doing all kinds of work for the US Navy, most of it still classified. Our age difference and our Air Force vs Navy background differences evaporated. Our well-matched, calm demeanors would be essential in the Persian Gulf when we led teams of workers preparing US Navy frigates and cruisers for combat in Desert Storm.

As the years went by, I took the same approach with Ray that had served me well when I was an Air Force officer working with senior enlisted people: tell them and show them that you value their deep experience. So, I ensured that Ray was recognized for everything that went well. Ray excelled at all tasks.

As manager, I learned to involve senior people in discussions and ask for their opinions. With the more experienced employees, I listened carefully to their ideas and took notes when they spoke. Be aware that, when you are a younger manager/supervisor of older people, they naturally assume you lack experience. Like it or not, you often must work to earn their respect. These tips will help you:

1. Be a low-drama person, not easily moved to excitement, hyperbole, or extreme words. Be authentic and genuine because people can sense a fake. Say nice things behind people's backs (the opposite of gossip) and mean them. It's bound to get back to them.

2. Build people skills. Show that you understand priorities and are working on the "big rocks first." If you need help, ask early. If it's people you need, have someone in mind and ask them and their boss for assistance. Demonstrate that you can gently manage jobs and lead colleagues in a way that makes them feel great about helping with any task. And here is something most managers forget, but the employees

never forget — people need enjoyment. Incorporate a little fun whenever possible. Lighten up. Make everyone feel valued. They will then want to help with future projects. Take periodic training classes to polish those skills.

3. Be present, consistent and have a good attitude. These characteristics appeal to people of all ages in the workforce. Arrive early for work (15 minutes will do it). Depart late from work each day. Complete and document every job you are assigned. Each ongoing job's progress should be tracked and visible. Keep a simple, weekly log and be happy at week's end when you have been consistent. Be aware of how people perceive you and the impression you leave. Everyone wants to be around happy people. Stay positive and refuse to think of yourself as a victim.

4. Show that you will do your share of crappy little jobs, without complaint. These are projects with little visibility for senior leadership and, consequently, are not needle-movers, financially, for the company. Grab these crappy jobs for two reasons: first, insignificant jobs let you spread your wings to try out new project management and people skills, and second you can fail at a few low-stakes PM efforts without hurting your career, especially if they are strictly internal. Chances are nobody will even notice. When you succeed, give other people some credit whenever you are congratulated for good work. When someone compliments a job you led, it just takes a second to reply, "That was a combined effort and Bob's team helped us get that launched" or "Thanks, but Evelyn and Steve were instrumental in making that come together on time."

5. Be flexible, even in job choices. If a new need arises for a position not yet "on the books," step up and take it yourself! Even if you are uncertain you can do the work without help! I have had several great jobs through the years that did not exist until I talked with a manager/team leader who said something like "We don't have the position you describe. . . but maybe we should!"

Example 2. I once received a wonderful job offer from a highly respected, growing R&D company, but I also had previously had casual conversations with another, smaller firm about working for them "someday." On the drive across town to accept the first offer, I stopped by the smaller firm to inform them of my new job. Their young president, who had been involved in those earlier, casual conversations, asked what I would be doing for the R&D

company, and I told him I would be the technical liaison who bridged the gap between the engineering staff and the DoD market for advanced sensors.

He responded with, "Well hell, Mack, we need that job done here too. What are they offering you?" Reluctantly (remember I am a Baby Boomer and salary/benefits information is compartmentalized in my brain), I told him my upcoming salary. He replied, "Have a seat in my office and let me talk with the Board of Directors for a few minutes." Ten minutes later, he came back with an offer of not only a salary 5% higher than the first firm offered, but a vice president position and company stock! I got my TS SCI clearance there and spent seven wonderful years working on amazing systems with friendly, honorable, technically proficient, professional people!

6. Get involved in something important. People like to work with visionaries. So become part of something larger than yourself: a religion, a social movement you really believe in, a family, a motorcycle club that rides for a social cause, or all the above. For me, that bigger thing has been bringing better systems to our Nation's Warfighters, faster and cheaper. Hang out with positive people who are proactive and feel good about themselves. And if you are sincere and committed, you will find kindred spirits who will join your cause!

7. Be determined to get along (cooperate and be professional) with everyone you meet. No matter how different you and they are. Learning to work with people who are different from yourself, as Ray was different from me, is a key skill. This entire area of soft skills is a tough one for many technical people. The additional challenges caused by age-differences—four generations simultaneously in the workplace—add to the difficulty of leading people. You must take this in stride. After all, if you were an American man raised on a cattle ranch in Texas, schooled at a southwestern engineering university, and your new boss was a French woman who studied archeology at Oxford, you would not expect her to see everything exactly the way you do, would you? You would be curious about the cultural differences and work with them. Age disparities are no different. A good team member expects differences, learns from them and enjoys the new perspectives.

I keep that piece of armor, and the bullet that hit Ray, on my desk. It reminds me every time I see it, that we need all the age groups working together, that each generation can learn from the others. As Ken Blanchard said, "None of Us is as Smart as All of Us."

Therefore:

- ➤ Control the impressions you leave with others. Do your job as well as possible, every time.

- ➤ Be dependable.

- ➤ Assess the ramifications of your words and actions, especially when heard and seen by different generations.

- ➤ Work constantly on your people skills.

- ➤ Have Truth-Tellers in your life and in your profession, who will give you their honest opinions.

- ➤ Maintain gentle pressure to improve in all areas and have some fun with friends and family along the way.

Chapter 3

Workplace Dynamics for the Project Leader

Rule 5: Demand (and Build) Superior Solutions

Rule 6: Look Beyond the Surface

Rule 7: Human Contact Connects People

Rule 8: Break the Bullying Cycle

Rule 9: Crush the Clique

Rule 5.   Demand (and Build) Superior Solutions

> Observation: Poorly designed systems and devices have become so commonplace that we have started to accept poorly functioning things as the norm.

We saw the "Do Not Flush" sign in a restroom at a restaurant. Surely, management did not mean for customers to also put *toilet paper in the trash can!* So that directive was simply wrong. Apparently, it had become the norm that people ignored the added "toilet paper" words on the sign and knew what management really wanted.

More than just an incorrect directive on a bathroom sign, this normalization of deviance is becoming commonplace in areas that really matter. It's destructive to society, lowers the frequency of excellent designs that we should be insisting upon, and damages a free-market meritocracy where the best ideas should generate the best designs and, therefore, the most profit.

Human-Systems Design (HSD) is finally getting the engineering attention it deserves in the systems engineering world. As humans, we all have some HSD capability and I encourage you to use those latent skills more often.

Example 1. We have all experienced frustration with a shop that has a glass door that must be pushed to open but has a handle for pulling. In *Seven Fundamental Design Rules*[7] Don Norman has identified many other problem-ridden systems and devices that we can improve. He talks about hundreds of everyday items with poor designs that are crying out for improvement such as the dishwasher that beeps loudly at 2 AM to tell you the cycle is finished, the cacophony of beeps and honks and flashing lights in an intensive care unit, and the sink stopper that lacks any obvious control and must be pressed to close and pressed again to open.

Example 2. In May 2023, this elevator control panel was sighted at a prestigious hospital complex in Maryland. Imagine you're late for a medical appointment and are told to go to the first floor.

---

[7] Don Norman, The Design of Everyday Things (Philadelphia: Basic Books, 2013) p 71, www.basicbooks.com

EMERGENCY PHONE

What button do you push? 01 or 1? Confusing, right?

What if you are told to meet someone on the second floor? Where is *that* button? It's missing.

Or if you are told to go to the Main floor, might you press the "M" button on the left, before you see the "1" button on the right with the red plate that says "Main"?

What a confusing floor numbering and naming system! Look at the photo again and think about how you could fix this in the easiest, least expensive way, then read our answer below.

First, a requirement: the numbers in black braille and the white switch buttons must be identical for each floor, to eliminate further confusion.

Now the solution: We can improve this panel with four new buttons: The lower two floors can be relabeled with G buttons, black and white, for Ground (instead of 01) and a plate that says Ground. The 2nd floor gets 2 black and white buttons (instead of 1) and no plate at all. The other floor buttons are fine. Unfortunately, all the office and suite numbers should also be changed to begin with the number of the floor they are on, all ground floor suites should be in the 100 series, all second floor suites should begin with the number 2, etc.

The least disruptive way to implement these changes would be to follow Sweden's example when they switched from driving on the left, to the right. They advertised the change extensively and printed new traffic signs. On September 3, 1967, the switchover simply happened, overnight. This hospital could do the same.

Therefore:

> ➢ **Train yourself and your teams to notice both poorly designed and well-designed systems.**

> ➢ **Examine closely the user interfaces and user experiences for devices that you enjoy using, to determine why they are easy to use.**

> ➢ **Think about how you can make your designs better, all the time.**

> ➢ **Keep your science-brain with you, even at the end of the day. The critical thinking used at work is necessary outside our work environments as well as in. Share your thinking with family and friends. Help make the world a better place.**

Rule 6.   Look Beyond the Surface

> Observation: Knowing a person's position on a topic is somewhat instructive but true insight comes from knowing their *interests*.

A person's mental position on a topic is their public standpoint about a subject. A person's interests are the deeper, often more emotional feelings about that subject. Spend minimal time discussing a person's positions. Build trust with the person and move quickly into their interests. This requires mutual trust.

Example 1: I was the Project Manager for an overseas assignment where I had several dozen US shipyard workers employed. One of those workers suddenly changed. His behavior became erratic, withdrawn and paranoid. His colleagues said he had always been a little odd and could become violent if provoked (see the "demons" discussion in *Rule 10*).

I "coincidentally" saw him on the pier where he worked and walked alongside him for a bit. I casually asked him how he was doing and how the job was going. He replied that all was well (his public position—be tough and keep that well-paying job). I told him he seemed nervous about something. It took me a few minutes of gentle prodding to break through and get to the real problem: his room was being "tossed" each day by the CIA while he was working. He was convinced he was being observed, had started carrying a razor knife "to defend himself" and was growing more anxious by the day. His real interest was just staying alive! In his mind, his life was in danger. I told him I would do some digging and get back to him right away, so we could form a plan to deal with the situation.

This put me in a tough spot. We barely had enough people to do the work and losing him could hurt our workflow. I consulted with our Project Manager and the Pier Supervisor who both said they could manage without him. I decided his paranoia was making him a danger to the other workers. (No, I did not even entertain for a moment the idea that his room WAS being searched by the CIA.)

I wanted to get him off the project and away from other people right away. Had I tried to convince him that it was most unlikely that the CIA was interested in this shipyard hourly worker from Long Beach, California, he would probably have transitioned to "well if not the CIA, then who IS doing it?" I was sure he was having a mental issue, so I did not argue with him.

I found him again that same afternoon and told him I had no information on intelligence agencies at work in his hotel. Then I said I was concerned for his safety in that Middle East country and asked him, "What do you think we should do?" He said he didn't know, and I sensed he was worried about what the rest of the crew would think if he left. But he was sincerely worried about being under surveillance, his room being searched, etc.

I did not bother telling him if professionals WERE searching his room, he would never see evidence of that, etc. Instead, I said, "If any group, government, gang or cartel or whoever, has taken an interest in you, 6,000 miles from the USA, let's not think about it too long—let's get you out of here!" I told him I would "square it" with the rest of the crew. He seemed relieved and I put him on the next flight to Europe that night with a connecting flight to his home station in Los Angeles.

Example 2. A US Air Force headquarters staff officer wrote a specification for a radar cable with requirements that included words to the effect, "The cable must have eight discreet, insulated copper conductors, must pass 256 kilobits/second of video signal from the radar to the operations shelter with a maximum signal loss of 2db, and must be 40 feet long, plus or minus 6 inches."

If that staff officer had had any hands-on experience with tactical radars, his *interests* would have been different and he would have added: "1. Should weigh less than 30 pounds so one person can carry it, and 2. Must connect securely and quickly on both ends, even with dirty threads, with no more than ¾ turn." That last change would have been just a few words in the contract and a few dollars more, but it could have meant life or death (*Rule 6*). The interests of end-users were not considered.

People will usually talk openly about their *positions* but are more guarded about their deeper *interests*. Getting to interests takes more time and requires a level of trust[8] between the parties. This is essential when laying out stakeholder matrices and documenting system requirements. While people may readily voice their positions, they are more likely to act on their interests.

Therefore:

> ➤ **Spend minimal time discussing a person's positions. Build trust with the person and move quickly into their interests.**

> ➤ **Take the time to talk with a broad spectrum of users and other stakeholders to capture their true needs and interests, not just their formal positions.**

> ➤ **Look at situations from the other person's point of view.**

---

[8] JV Venable, "Breaking the Trust Barrier" (Oakland, CA: Berrett-Koehler Publishers, 2016). JV refers to interests as *passions*, but the concept is the same — an underlying motivator. On page 71 in JV's excellent book, he and I stress the importance of establishing trust, so people feel comfortable sharing their interests with you.

Rule 7.   Human Contact Connects People

> Observation: Humans have a biological need to be touched by friendly human hands. However, we live in an increasingly digital age that creates a barrier to human contact.

There is a power when people touch each other. Unfortunately, virtual meetings and communications dominate the business world. This saves time and money, but reduces human contact with its myriad advantages:

1. **Closer psychological connections**: humans build closer, higher bandwidth connections with other humans during face-to-face meetings than with any other kind of interactions.

2. **Nonverbal communications**: video cameras are not ideal for capturing the full spectrum of human tells, the nonverbal cues and messages we all emit subconsciously. Some estimates are that 70% of communications involves nonverbal processes. Video cameras capture only a tiny fraction of those cues during virtual meetings.

3. **Handshakes**: The custom of shaking hands waxes and wanes, often driven by the virus de jour and our efforts to control spread. But the business handshake and the customs surrounding it are still important tools for establishing and maintaining rapport between people. Handshakes, speaking distances, and local customs are important tools for every professional. Learn various handshaking techniques. Practice them.

4. **Social cues**: Reading the room and deciding with whom you will speak and when are important tools for every leader. Be in-person to make use of these tools. Our brains are hardwired to interface with humans.

Example 1. I worked in Virginia for a supervisor whose office was in a western state. I only saw him during our annual all-hands meetings when I traveled out west to attend them. We repeatedly invited him to come east but he never visited our Virginia office during the four years I worked for him. He once attended a conference less than an hour's drive from us, yet he couldn't be bothered to stop by and meet our customer at DISA at Ft. Meade nor the eight employees who served him. And he never got to meet our Aberdeen Proving Ground customers and the dozens of our employees there. It was a lost opportunity for our supervisor and our company, and sadly it was tolerated by his boss. The damage his four-plus-years of absence caused our relationships at DISA and Aberdeen is incalculable. We lost a major, follow-on contract at Aberdeen a few months later. Would face-to-face discussions there, and some human contact in a few handshakes, have made a difference? Would we have learned *why* we were about to lose that upcoming competition? We will never know.

Example 2. NATO Study Group 79 for non-traditional electronic intelligence studies rotated the quarterly meeting location among the nine nations represented. Video teleconferences would have been much cheaper and easier but not nearly as effective in getting people to work together. Dr. G. Winterling, the study lead, kept the multi-national team focused on working together and delivering a solid, actionable study report by rotating the meeting location each month, so each nation's participants could entertain the group and show hospitality. More importantly, the dinners every evening and the face-to-face conversations welded us, *individuals,* into a study team.

Example 3. A Marine Gunnery Sergeant once told me about the reaction a just-wounded troop exhibits when touched by a friendly human. He described the typical 19-year-old Marine who is in combat for the first time and gets wounded: in pain, terrified and near shock. Then, when a buddy or the medic touches that person—lays a hand anywhere on him—the result is often miraculous. The rapid breathing slows, the heart rate slows, the blood pressure changes, and the person visibly relaxes.

All humans, and not just those wounded in battle, are wired to respond positively to a friendly touch.

Therefore:

➢ **Do not fight your hardwired brain: meet regularly in person with employees and customers. Travel regularly to meet your direct reports wherever they are. Go with them to meet key customers.**

➢ **Resist the tendency to meet virtually and lead remotely. Force yourself, even when swamped with work, to get out and physically meet with remote members on the project. Be old-school in meeting face-to-face with teammates.**

➢ **Establish trust. Shake hands with people. Just remember unwanted touching can be offensive and can lead to the termination of your employment. Be professional and respect personal space.**

Rule 8.   Break the Bullying Cycle

Observation: Bullying people destroys productivity and can scar victims for life.

Those who behave arrogantly or unfairly toward other people exhibit signs of being a bully. Physically intimidating other people is another sign. Emotionally manipulating people is bullying behavior. The best way to respond is to refuse to allow others to run over you. However, bullies do not like resistance so be prepared for push-back. In the workplace this can result in arguments or even physical altercations. However, it's imperative for you to stand up for yourself. Maintaining a positive self-image is important for your mental and physical health and your performance at work.

Example 1. Many years ago in Virginia, I was thinking about selling a classic convertible that I had restored. A man nicknamed "Moose" showed interest. I met with him in a sketchy part of Newport News, Virginia. He was brusque, had a heavy New York or New Jersey accent and an aggressive, arrogant demeanor. I know it's a cliché but I was a naïve West Virginian boy and I remember thinking, "this is guy has mafia written all over him." We met at his friend's business office where Moose said to me, "If my wife likes the car, I'll pay cash," and he flashed the cash, a fat wad of 100 dollar bills. I thought to myself, "yes, probably marked bills from a bank robbery!" I said, "I'd rather have a check please." He responded aggressively, "You'll get cash."

That loud response shocked me, but I was intimidated and said nothing. He loaned me his late-model Corvette for the weekend while he took my Mercedes home to see if his wife liked it. She didn't like the standard shift (duh - - - it was a classic 1958 109 SL) so the next Monday we swapped keys again, and that was that. I am embarrassed to say, the episode has haunted me for decades. Now, being older and less tolerant of bullies, my response today would be to tell him I had changed my mind, the car was not for sale, and just walk away. For over forty years, I rented a tiny amount of space in my head to that bully. I wish I hadn't.

Example 2. Years ago, I had just started working with a company and was attending a low-key dinner. The Vice President for Business Development was sitting next to me and we were chatting about something. He suddenly said, "Stop talking" and went about munching on his salad. I was shocked but stopped talking and he continued chewing. I was confused since he did not immediately start a conversation with anyone else at the table. The dinner continued, he never mentioned his odd directive to me, and I remained perplexed by the whole thing. A few weeks later, I saw him exhibit raw arrogance toward other people in other conversations and I concluded that he had been simply "putting me in my place" at the restaurant. He did not want to listen to someone else speak. He didn't have any other reason for showing bad manners—he was just bullying the new guy so he would know his place.

Therefore:

> ➤ **Do not let bullies damage your self-image. You do not have to argue with them. You can usually say "we can discuss this later" or "we are not going to agree on this issue." Then walk away.**

> ➤ **Guard against inadvertently bullying others. Periodically ask people you trust if your mannerisms, tone of voice or choice of words could reasonably be misconstrued as bullying.**

> ➤ **Be especially cautious about publicly confronting any porcupine-like, prickly bully who begins to meet the criteria for a sociopath. See *Rule 21*.**

> ➤ **Treat coworkers and direct reports respectfully, as if you were all members of a voluntary group. Should anyone become unhappy with your actions, expect them to leave.**

Rule 9.   Crush the Clique

Observation: Informal gangs will sometimes single out someone who is different or a threat to their interests.

Mobbing other people is industrial strength bullying by a group of people, usually targeting someone viewed as outside their clique. Some miscreants lack the courage to bully people one-on-one. Instead, when several of these degenerates see another person as different or threat, they become an informal group and begin to *cooperate* in pushing their targeted person around.

This is mobbing and it can be insidious. It may start as negative comments about the person's ideas. Then the mob may purposively exclude the target from business or social functions. Mobbing may also appear in the form of severe criticism of the target's design or suggestion.

This behavior is contagious. If a group singles out one individual for mistreatment, someday they may single YOU out. It's just plain wrong. A senior person must put a stop to this at once. Otherwise, the quality of the organization's product or service will be adversely affected, team cohesion will be destroyed, and stronger, more divisive cliques are likely to form. If it cannot be stopped and you have the authority, reassign the instigators. If it continues, fire them and reassign the targeted person to a different area or project, before a lawsuit is filed.

Example 1. A close family friend was working for the Swiss government when a group of younger colleagues took a dislike to him. They became a kind of mob, determined to get him forced out, reassigned or demoted. This guy was an experienced electrical engineer with decades of experience on international radar and electronic warfare (EW) programs. The mob "forgot" to invite him to key meetings, belittled his inputs in the meetings he did attend, and openly snickered when he spoke. He was mystified as to why they were doing this but he went to his management, described the behaviors he was seeing and identified the people involved. His management put a stop to it immediately.

Example 2. I personally experienced mobbing while working at a mid-sized engineering company for a short time. I was not part of the "in" crowd and they came after me. I was the new Director of Marketing at this company and I knew I would have an uphill battle to get accepted: I was the only member of the nine-person executive team who was neither a former employee of a certain, well-known radar firm nor a graduate of that firm's radar engineering program. In fact, I had been working at the competition for 16 years! Foolishly, I thought that experience made me valuable to this employer. Wrong! I had joined a cult without knowing it.

At an all-hands meeting, I briefed the entire company on my approach to business development. Among many other things, I talked about the importance of our field engineers listening to our customers and getting comments and suggestions about our products back to me and the business development team.

An hour after that all-hands session, a senior engineer sent me a personal email that said "I took a poll of the engineers here and they said you make way too much sense, are too competent, and your fresh approach will not be well received by the CEO and leadership clique that runs this place. We give you 18 months working here before you get frustrated and leave." I called him and told him he was mistaken. I was there to stay.

But he was right! I got mobbed. Within a few months, I noticed I was no longer being invited to all the strategy sessions with the CEO. The CEO became confrontational with me. I was being left off key emails. And my direct reports became distant and uncommunicative. I was miserable. I lasted 18 months before I resigned. I later learned that I was the 6th Marketing Director the firm had hired and lost in the previous 7 years! I wish I had known that before I took the job. I had not done my homework thoroughly enough nor early enough. Shame on me.

Example 3. In a large engineering corporation where I worked, we had an excellent engineer who suffered from Tourette's Syndrome. The condition caused him to blurt out words and phrases that should never be uttered in a professional setting. He would do this in briefings, customer meetings, in hallways, wherever he happened to be. He had no control over this impulse. While it made for some amusing situations, when he did this around customers or other visitors who did not know him, one of his colleagues would quietly explain, "That's just Oscar (not his real name). He has Tourette's. Pay no attention."

He made great engineering contributions to many national defense projects. Nowadays, in our increasingly hyper-politically-correct world, I suspect emotionally immature colleagues might find a way to mob and push aside talented but non-ordinary people like Oscar. That would be a shame.

Being "different" does not have to be as extreme as Oscar's case to require special handling by an organization's leadership. Again some sage words from Noel Longuemare:[9]

> *Quite often there are very bright but unique individuals who are non-conformists or "odd balls" that do not fit in with the more "normal" employees. A really good manager has the ability to discover these people, ascertain what special talents they may have, and then create an environment that allows those to flourish, even when the individual may have some other traits that are not stellar. I [once knew] an engineer who worked as a real loner and was not embraced by the rest of his group. He was considered a wild man and severely criticized by others. However, after showing him that his work was valuable and giving him some slack, he designed an amazing device that most experts felt was impossible, and it became a major feature of a key surveillance system.*
>
> *Almost every individual has something of value to contribute, but they may be terrible at some other things. A common problem is that some very capable people are put in positions they are not cut-out for, and then demoted/terminated when they inevitably fail. This is really not their fault as much as the management that put them in the wrong job. This happens more often than you might expect. The most frequent example is putting a highly capable technical person in charge of managing a group or project when they totally lack management skills (or desire). A really good manager finds ways to place people in positions where they can exploit their strengths and DOES NOT require them to do things they are not good at.*

---

[9] Noel Longuemare is former Principal Deputy Undersecretary of Defense for Acquisition and Technology at the Pentagon under President Bill Clinton, where he was responsible for the U.S. Department of Defense's (DoD) $100 billion acquisition budget. He also served as Acting Under Secretary of Defense. I knew Noel at Westinghouse Defense where he worked both before and after his stint with the USG.

Therefore:

➤ Watch for mobbing of employees and put a stop to it quickly.

➤ Resist being lured into joining a mob. If a clique to which you already belong begins to feel exclusionary, leave it.

➤ Find ways to retain and fully utilize slightly odd people. When you get older, you may be one.

➤ Tolerate the minor quirks of high-performing contributors. And protect them from other less-understanding employees.

Chapter 4

Secrets for Effective Leadership

Rule 10: Take the High Road

Rule 11: Coach Constantly or Kiss Them Goodbye

Rule 12: The Boss is Wrong. Now What?

Rule 13: Successful Projects Are Never Easy

Rule 14: Get Your Hands Dirty

Rule 15: Words Echo Forever

Rule 10. Take the High Road

Observation: People detest hypocrites. Truly effective leaders exemplify professionalism by leading by example and demonstrating authentic behavior they expect to see in others.

How do leaders walk the high road and not tumble off? They learn to act as an objective professional in all situations. Then, as a professional, they constantly demonstrate that they know how to take care of their direct reports, their projects, their organization and themselves.

Example 1. A colleague makes a snarky remark to a team leader or colleague in public. The professional remains calm and may suggest a private chat to discuss the incident without getting upset or showing emotion. They may ask, "Why would you say something like that?"

Example 2. A team leader is driving colleagues to a meeting and another driver cuts him off. The professional responds with calm tolerance. He lets the incident go without reaction. It may sound silly but when driving with colleagues in the car, professionals let other vehicles pass when needed. They drive calmly and defensively. A professional is low ego, not easily angered and stays focused on the task of defensive driving.

Example 3. Your boss sends out a poorly worded email or makes an unprofessional comment in a virtual meeting. You and other employees heard it. Later, while talking with your colleagues, a professional knows not to say anything about the boss that they would not say to the boss. They would not say, "What the hell got into the boss this morning?" If anything, they would say "That was out of character. The boss must be under some stress these days." Or similar. They speak as if everything they say will get back to the boss, because it might. A reasoned response or no response at all demonstrates the professional's emotional maturity and calm demeanor.

So, when you see something or someone behaving oddly, do not be judgmental. Instead, be curious and ask yourself, "What are they wrestling with internally that could cause that behavior?" This is the reaction you would want to see from others if it had been you who lost your temper in public.

Strive to develop a curious mindset about everything. This is how entrepreneurs are wired. A hallmark of good leaders is also the ability to develop a vision for a better future by constantly asking themselves "how could we make that better?" They seek to move past positions to get to interests. (*Rule 6*)

What can Ted Lasso™ teach us about leading teams? In an episode in the British series, Ted is challenged to a dart game in a pub. Ted says, "a person can be either curious about things and people, or judgmental." So, make up your mind right now, as you read this *Rule*, to be curious in life, rather than judgmental. Be curious about everything and everyone.

How do you do this? Well, train yourself to react to any adverse event or undesirable comment with a mindset that asks, "hmm, I wonder why that is?" rather than, "that is terrible." This may be hard to do at first because gut-reacting in a judgmental way is easy and somehow enjoyable. It often consists of mentally putting the perpetrator into a "box" with a label, and then saying or thinking something derogatory about that entire group. Do not do it. This is closely akin to "Identity Politics" where people are first grouped based on some characteristic or trait and then *marginalized*. Do not let yourself fall into that lazy way of thinking.

When you see a task being done inefficiently or some other inexplicable behavior, ask yourself, "what could be causing this" and "how could this be improved?" Keep an open mind regarding solutions to vexing problems because answers come from unexpected places. When someone behaves badly toward me, I try to remain calm and think to myself, "Many people are dealing with personal demons that the rest of us cannot even begin to imagine."

Even when you are appropriately curious, do not pat yourself on the back for being correct. Never allow yourself to become arrogant.

> . . . *discover where your intellectual arrogance is causing disabling ignorance and overcome it. Far too many people, especially people with great expertise in one area, are contemptuous of knowledge in other areas or believe that being bright is a substitute for knowledge. First-rate engineers, for instance, tend to take pride in not knowing anything about people. Human beings, they believe, are much too disorderly for the engineering mind. Human resources professionals, by contrast, often pride themselves on their ignorance of elementary accounting or of quantitative*

methods altogether. Taking pride in such ignorance is self-defeating. Go to work on acquiring the skills and knowledge you need to fully realize your strengths.[10]

Collaboration and professionalism go hand in hand. Each requires looking at issues objectively, not emotionally or subjectively. Since we live in a project-based economy, people are already somewhat pre-wired with the basic skills to cooperate with other people and, when needed, can tap into them. Anthropologists believe this collaboration in brain wiring, enhanced by rudimentary language skills, enabled Early Modern Humans to out-populate Neanderthals. There it is—you are hard-wired to work well with others!

Therefore:

> ➤ Take the high road and be professional by leading by example. It's not dangerous up there — you will not fall off!

> ➤ Demonstrate patience with others in all that you do, professionally and privately, so it becomes a habit.

> ➤ Be curious, not judgmental — this makes you approachable (unlike a porcupine!).

> ➤ Collaborate and continue to refine your collaboration skills, tools and processes.

> ➤ Develop a calm demeanor and surround yourself with like-minded people.

---

[10] "Managing Oneself," Peter F. Drucker, Best of HBR 1999, Harvard Business Review, January 2005, pages 3 and 6. Reprints available at customerservice@harvardbusiness.org.

Rule 11. Coach Constantly or Kiss Them Goodbye

> Observation: Every person in every organization deserves to be mentored and coached sufficiently.

Managers are entrusted with the care and feeding of an organization's most priceless asset, its people.

Competent, well-trained supervisors know how to mentor their direct reports and have a fair and objective system in place to evaluate them on a regular basis. This mentoring/evaluation session should happen formally at least quarterly. Coaching may also be occasionally sprinkled into casual, private interactions. An evaluation should not only highlight areas where their direct reports rock, they must also identify areas where they need to make changes. The most helpful part of the evaluation is the review of the career progression plan for that particular employee. This is when the manager gives advice and encourages the employee to take the steps necessary to advance their careers.

If you are a supervisor, always provide rationale and specific changes you want to see. If your direct reports are also supervisors, you must also confirm that their people are being coached/mentored. This confirmation must be a part of your direct reports' quarterly reviews. Also to be included: Who is being groomed for which positions? Who needs more exposure to senior leadership? Who needs more training?

Example 1. In the days of "waterfall" or "big bang" software development, Ross Perot's company, EDS, invested in thorough training for newly hired software developers. Each programmer's performance was closely tracked and became a topic in quarterly reviews, so people regularly learned when and where they needed to improve. Newly-trained EDS programmers with one year experience averaged 5% failure rates, compared to 40-year-old software engineers at a major defense company, without the training, who suffered failure rates averaging 40%.

Example 2. Good leaders and managers coach and mentor by first getting to know their people. They do that by practicing MBWA—Management By Wandering/Walking Around. MBWA refers to a style of management which involves managers maintaining an active presence throughout all corners of the workplace to interact with employees in an unscheduled, ad hoc manner.

When the manager is fully engaged in what is going on in the workplace first-hand, a wide range of benefits ensue. Try it out.

My close colleagues and I practice MBWA as much as possible and we always learn from the interactions.

> *I feel this [MBWA] is an unusually effective and powerful tool, and I tried to apply it in my own career. One of my instructors at the Stanford Executive Program … told the following story: "A very successful businessman and manager gave a lecture about the merits of this approach. After it was over, a young manager came up and asked him how he found time to walk around. He said, "Sir, after I get through with the staff meeting and attend all the other meetings and similar demands, I don't have time to walk around. How do you do it?" The older man replied: "Well, after I finish walking around, I sometimes have time for the staff meeting and other demands." It helps to get one's priorities right.*
>
> *—Noel Longuemare*

Therefore:

➢ Set up a regular rhythm of coaching and mentoring of your direct reports. Meet and talk with each of your people at least quarterly and preferably monthly. If they are matrixed to you, you will share this responsibility with their direct supervisor and the issues you will address will be more project related.

➢ Begin mentoring sessions with the employee talking, perhaps answering questions about what is going well, challenges they are tackling, and other issues. Be dedicated to helping your employees excel at their work, a more important role than "supervising" their output. Select training courses with them that will build their skills. Ask them to share key lessons learned with the whole staff.

➢ Establish annual 360-degree assessments whereby every employee and manager is evaluated anonymously by several managers above their level in the firm, by several peers and by several direct reports. Recognize that these assessments can be earth-shaking experiences for those who have not participated in them before.

➢ Incorporate feedback into opportunities for the employees to advance by offering resources and additional training.

➢ Practice MBWA, alone if possible. Hold in strict confidence everything you hear or learn. Refrain from using the information you collect to punish or chastise anyone later, even gently, otherwise that will be your last productive MBWA session! Refrain from directly offering to fix problems you hear about, since that can destroy the organizational structure. Sanitize what you have learned so the origins cannot be traced back to the people you spoke with during your MBWA sessions.

Rule 12. The Boss is Wrong! Now What?

> Observation: We trust our bosses. When people above us in rank or position suggest we do something, most of us just do it.

"OK, boss, I'll get right on it." might be a correct response to a boss, or it can be catastrophic.

> *Most of the time when an employee disagrees with the boss, the employee lacks the big picture of the strategy and other tasks underway to achieve the goals. A professional will learn to request a private meeting with the boss and respectfully discuss their concerns behind closed doors. If the boss shares additional information that puts the task in context of the larger effort, the next step is easy. The employee performs the task wholeheartedly. If the boss continues along the same lines but does not share inside information, the next step may seem harder, but assuming that what the boss wants is legal and moral, the employee should shut up and do it. Otherwise, the employee should look for a new job.*
>
> *—Colonel Bill Brei, USAF, Ret.*

To emphasize the above, if the boss is asking you to do something within the best interests of the organization and it's legal, just do it or seek other employment. If it's illegal, immoral, or unethical, that is a different thing entirely. Let your conscience be your guide. But when the boss is wrong and lives are at stake, speak up!

Example 1. A leader doing it wrong in "Desert One." In 1979, the US president is said to have inserted himself personally into the military planning of an ill-fated raid to free American hostages being held by Iran, contributing to the failure of the rescue mission. President Jimmy Carter had previously "dismantled the CIA's network of spies due to the agency's role in overthrowing governments in Vietnam and Latin America" which further eroded our intelligence capabilities in advance of that raid.[11]

---

[11] https://www.airforcemag.com/article/0199desertone/

Although Carter was under political pressure to do something about the American hostages, he personally refused to allow the US military to conduct a crucial reconnaissance flight over Iran to find a suitable staging site for a rescue raid for fear if discovered it might impact ongoing State Department negotiations with the Iranians.

A person directly involved in that raid explained to me that, contrary to a publicly released article, Carter himself decided on the small number of RH-53D Navy helicopters (helos) to be used in the raid.

This number was far short of that recommended by the professional mission planners. [12] Col. Charles Beckwith wanted ten helos, the Navy said it could launch only eight from the USS Nimitz for the mission, and six were the minimum number needed to haul the American hostages. What happened? There was poor planning by a team scattered around the globe, mistrust of intelligence sources, radio failures, shifting weather, swapping of helicopter crews, poorly maintained helos and aircraft systems failures. When mechanical problems reduced the eight helicopters to seven, then six and finally five, the mission was aborted.

While leaving the desert staging base, a helicopter hovering in blowing sand slid into a parked C-130 cargo aircraft full of fuel. The resulting inferno killed five airmen and three marines. The end result is now history: a failed raid, eight American servicemen killed, the American government looking like a bunch of idiots, the 1986 Goldwater-Nichols DOD Reorganization Act that

---

[12] The truth may be lost in history. An article in the New York Times by Zbigniew Brzezinski did not eliminate the possibility of a personal decision by Carter regarding the insufficient number of helicopters, but I cannot find further confirmation of that allegation.

redefined the power structure of the Pentagon, and the birth of the Special Operations Command (SOCOM) to prevent non-special-operations people from ever again planning special forces operations.

Example 2. A leader doing it right—Dr. Gerhard Winterling was a low-ego, patient team leader and Chair of NATO Study Group 79. I was Deputy Chair of that group, and I watched him adroitly lead a team of engineers from nine nations through a multi-year study. Several times I thought his easy-going attitude was causing unneeded delays in our project as he took hours to smooth ruffled feathers and encourage collaboration among the nation's respective representatives. I was in a fix: If I did not speak up, the study could overrun its schedule and we would not deliver our report as agreed. If I did speak up, I could insult the intelligence of my boss, Dr. Winterling.

I decided the viability of the study effort, which was likely to be essential to the defensive posture of several nations, outweighed any interpersonal strife my concern might trigger between Dr. Winterling and myself. So, I quietly voiced that concern to him. He listened patiently, told me he had thought of that possibility but that he had secretly plugged-in almost 30 days of extra time in our original schedule for just that kind of schmoozing (plus weathered-out meetings, sickness and replacement of key people, etc.). His thinking was way ahead of mine. Over the next 16 months, he continued to take time to massage the egos of each participant so they stayed engaged. He joked a lot and kept things light to minimize the effects of historical animosities (the British and French participants did NOT get along). He kept our focus on the technical issues and operational challenges. And he was exactly right: the result was a masterfully assembled study, delivered on time! I did the final editing on our report. It was packed with solid findings and technical recommendations and backed by well-supported analysis. As importantly, it welded together disparate professionals, many with hidden agendas and "marching orders," into a close-knit *NATO group*. And that does not happen often.

Dr. Winterling, who passed away a few years ago, was a great boss and an empathetic team leader. Although I occasionally disagreed with him on minor points, I am glad I did what he asked and remained patient. Watching him take the time to listen to each participant and get the British and French engineers to nominally work together taught me a lot about leading teams of disparate talents and widely varying national perspectives. When you are faced with multicultural challenges, remember the sage, worldly techniques of Dr. Winterling. You can do it!

Example 3. Me, almost doing it wrong. The *You Only Live Once (YOLO)* mindset should always be tempered with the thought of what could happen if things go wrong, also known as the "What-If" exercise.

I was visiting a European air-traffic control facility to discuss equipment with my host, a General officer I had known from a class we attended years earlier. I had once been an active radar controller but had not done that job for years. It felt good to be back.

It was the evening shift at the radar facility. We put on headsets to listen to air traffic radio conversations. My General officer friend turned to me and casually said, "Mack, tell Lufthansa 3564 to descend from flight level 220 to flight level 200."

I had directed altitude changes to pilots thousands of times as an active controller, but I hadn't issued that directive to any pilot in almost two decades. I chuckled and expressed confused gratitude, asking him why he wanted me to do that. He said, "Somebody has to descend that flight and one of the other controllers will have do it if you don't. Have a little fun."

I thought about it for a moment and imagined what a good story it would make for my grandchildren. Then I remembered I was not a certified air traffic controller in Europe (or anywhere else at that point). I was in that ATC facility solely as a civilian, with no authority to direct air traffic.

This was a prickly situation: If I refused, I might look cowardly to the other controllers there that night, and it might insult my gracious host. On the other hand, if I acquiesced and something went wrong . . .

My "What-If" training kicked in to protect me. If, for any reason, air traffic control authorities needed to review the audio tapes from that evening (and this happens frequently in those organizations) they would hear an American voice giving a command to a civilian airliner flying over Europe! That would violate multiple international laws and regulations and could come back to bite me!

I thanked my old classmate and declined. It would have stoked my ego, been a great once-in-a-lifetime opportunity, and made a great story, but the risks outweighed the benefits. It would have been the wrong thing to do.

During your career, you will face similar decisions. Consult the correct moral code (you are building that code now, by the way) and play the What-If game in your head. You will make the right choices.

Therefore:

> ➢ **Seek a private meeting with your boss if you believe following the boss' direction is either illegal, immoral or will hurt the organization.**

> ➢ **Respect the boss' position. You like being employed, right?**

> ➢ **Play the "What-If" game constantly and always consider not just the likelihood of a bad outcome for a decision, but also the magnitude of that outcome. Think about the chance of having a car accident driving to a nearby grocery store, which may be low but not zero, so you have auto insurance. Listen to the tiny voice in your head that whispers "what if the worst happens ..." because this is your career insurance.**

> ➢ **Choose your battles wisely; do not join the club of unemployed people whose last words were "Hold my beer ..."**

Rule 13. Successful Projects Are NEVER Easy

| Observation: Everything seems easy to people who have never done it.

It's tempting at times to involve small, perhaps newly launched companies in your projects: They often cost less and are easier to work with than larger, better-established firms. But they may be rookies! Your project/program may look easy to them because they have never tackled anything quite like it. Of course, everyone needs to *[insert your favorite trite phrase here: learn the ropes, cut their teeth, etc.]* but I prefer to have inexperienced companies learn on someone else's defense projects that are funded with taxpayers' money, NOT on my projects!

Example 1. Consider the Phoenix drone system developed for the UK military. According to our research and our discussions with SpyFlight[13] people in the United Kingdom, the British Army needed to see how close to their targets their ground-launched missiles were actually hitting. They wanted a large, airborne drone to snap pictures of the battlefield, at roughly a hundred miles range from the British missile launch units, and transmit the pictures via radio back to the missile-targeting crews.

They could have chosen to buy the American MQ-1 Predator drone which was already in widespread use, or any number of other, non-developmental drones. Instead, perhaps out of national pride and an imperative to help a struggling aircraft development industry, the British government decided to design and build a new drone themselves. Unfortunately, at that time the UK government lacked the expertise to design an entire drone system, especially an air vehicle that could do the job needed.

To make matters worse, the British contractor to whom the government awarded the prime contract had never built an aircraft, nor had the subcontractor chosen by that prime ever built an air vehicle. The results are sad: a system that took about 11 years to get fully fielded, by which time the British Army's needs for the drone had changed completely (color video

---

[13] https://spyflight.co.uk/uav/#Phoenix

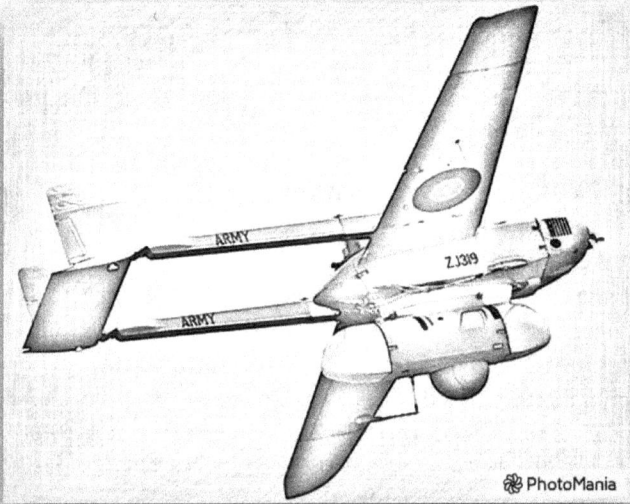

cameras instead of black and white still pictures, six hours of time needed in the air instead of two hours, etc.).

This was an acquisition disaster. The aircraft engine they chose overheated in the desert environment. The aircraft was launched from a rail atop a military truck but the truck the government chose would not fit into the only tactical cargo aircraft the British had at the time, the C-130 Hercules. Nor would that same truck fit through the Chunnel under the English Channel, so it could not be driven off the British Isles to France where it could be shipped further by rail or road. It had to be deployed by slow ship or by hitchhiking a ride on an American C-17 or other large cargo aircraft. Hitchhiking is an unreliable way to get anyplace, right?

There was no provision for conventional landing gear on the aircraft, which tells us there was little if any aeronautical design engineering experience on the British government team, so the landing solution finally chosen was a scabbed-on parachute. Even that butt-ugly arrangement took seven years to mature sufficiently for fielding. We have beaten up the poor Phoenix team enough. In the end, what should have cost approximately USD $250K per air vehicle, actually cost the UK taxpayer the equivalent of $2.25M each.

Example 2. A colleague and I watched a Middle Eastern company import and export expensive goods and it didn't look too complex to us: Customs experts handled goods coming through the ports, a bank handled letters of credit, and the owners raked in lots of profits! Sometimes, the trading company did not even need to take title to the goods — they just put the deals together and made a fat commission.

So we launched Southern Trading Company. It was a Chapter S corporation and there were three of us as founders and officers. Now all we had to do was find US buyers in need of foreign goods, and vice versa. We planned to rely on the US Foreign and Commercial Service (USFCS) representatives in US Embassies worldwide for outreach into their respective nations. But that was the flaw in our plan: In those days, the foreign-based USFCS people we talked to on the phone from the US East Coast were useless. They offered some canned service-levels to promote US products and services at trade fairs, but they did not do individual outreach for US companies. We had thought their services would be like those of their counterparts in British Embassies we had known, whose commercial people were truly advocates, meeting prospective clients for UK firms, arranging introductions, involving the country's defense department when necessary, etc.

We offered innovative, lightweight body armor and several other US products. We dabbled in steel re-bar out of Eastern Europe, and even tried to broker deals in rice, sugar and gold. During a two-day lay-over in Hong Kong, I once personally contacted the Hong Kong police department (in the UK-Hong Kong days, before it was ceded to China) regarding our client's American body armor. I faxed the main office from my hotel and they didn't respond. They wouldn't even take a meeting with me.

Operating an Import-Export company looked easy from the outside. It was anything but! In the days before the Internet, people looked to known friends and associates for business connections. Unfortunately, we were not in anyone's Rolodex of contacts for the commodities that were being so frequently traded internationally. We could sometimes find a buyer, but no supplier would trust us to make the deal. Or vice versa. It was the old adage "People do business with people they trust". Nobody in that business knew us, so nobody would trust us. We closed the company.

Therefore:

- ➤ Recognize when something is too hard for your team to solve or too large for its budget. Do your homework!

- ➤ Study the success stories of design experts such as Kelly Johnson and Ben Rich who built impossible aircraft.

- ➤ Team with winners. Examine the past performance of potential subcontractors or teammates. Note if there are significant numbers of unhappy users, late deliveries, budget overruns or court cases. Find those who can deliver.

- ➤ Avoid subcontractors with bad reputations or without significant domain experience, who want to work on your project.

- ➤ Talk to end-users as much as practical to get their real interests pushed into designs.

- ➤ Hire experts when you need them on your team, and find them wherever you must.

Rule 14. Get Your Hands Dirty

Observation: To understand the nuances of utility, training, maintenance or other support of any device or system, there is no substitute for the designers getting hands-on experience.

You can repeatedly tell a jet engine manufacturer's leadership that their designs should always allow enough space between components so that a mechanic's gloved hand holding a wrench can fit between the components. Letting the corporate executive experience some frustration is even better, especially if that frustration involves the exec's own hand, on a B-52's engine, in the snow, on a flight line in North Dakota, in January!

Example: The US Air Force "Blue Two" program did exactly that. The program successfully paired defense industry executives with Air Force mechanics who worked on that defense company's equipment. As a Westinghouse Operations Engineer, I participated in Blue Two for environmental remediation and saw first-hand how effective it is to bring design and engineering people to the field to give them new perspectives.

Maintenance seems to have taken a back seat in defense system development over the past 20 years. For example, aircrew members' opinions and suggestions are routinely considered during systems design work, but suggestions about the practical details of hands-on maintenance and repair are not always solicited. For hardware, Computer Aided Design and Manufacturing and Augmented Reality are bringing improvements to

maintenance-driven design but more emphasis is needed. For software related work, designers must fully understand the customer's normal, cyber-compliant operating procedures for patches, upgrades and updates, and ensure their new system can be maintained. The customer should not be forced to change the way they normally do routine things just to suit the software of a new system, unless that new system is transformative and intended to entirely change what people have been doing.

Project Managers and Team Leaders, make sure your developers talk to the end customer and fully understand the customer's wants and needs. Be sure the needed travel and interaction is in the budget.

Therefore:

➤ **Expose engineers to field operations, especially maintenance, early in their careers and early again in each development project.**

➤ **Seek opportunities for engineers and other professionals to attend exercises or demonstrations where their systems and competitors' systems are being used so they can learn first-hand about capabilities, limitations, and needed improvements. In defense companies, employees who are also members of the Reserves or Air/National Guard can be instrumental in making these opportunities happen for their corporate colleagues.**

Rule 15. Words Echo Forever

> Observation: Words can create psychological wounds in other people, wounds that never heal. Words can be completely misinterpreted.

As supervisors, coaches and mentors, your words carry lots of weight. We all know, and probably have experienced, the wounds that words can make. We have felt the sting of an insult or a lie and many of those stings can last a lifetime. Much has been written about the lasting power of words. I want to talk about a different kind of problem with words: the scrambling of an entire phrase's meaning between when it's spoken and when it's registered and understood in the listener's mind. No matter how carefully we *choose* them, our words may not be heard exactly the way we intend. I have seen this happen several times and it always surprises me.

Example. I once lived in a residential community where the streets were connected to an active airfield. We residents kept aircraft at our homes and taxied out to the runway, via the streets, whenever we liked. Thus our streets doubled as taxiways. After I moved in, I noticed we had no warning signs on our streets. It was not long before I was taxiing our Cessna 182 toward the runway at our adjacent airport and encountered a tourist in a car, head-on toward me on our main street. I could not leave the aircraft to ask them to pull into someone's driveway so I could continue. I could not back-up the aircraft. Finally, after several minutes of me gesturing for them to pull off the taxiway and both my engine and body temperatures climbing, the wayward motorist figured it out and moved out of the way.

At the next meeting of the Homeowners Association, I recounted the incident. Other pilots told similar tales. We had all seen signs in other airparks with warnings such as "Beware of taxiing aircraft" and "Parents, spinning props kill! Keep your children away from aircraft." We had no such signs posted and no gates on our streets. This led many motorists to think ours were public access roads.

The HOA Board of Directors agreed that we should post a few warning signs. A fellow pilot and I volunteered to choose the wording for the signs.

Cal (not his real name) and I met the next Saturday over coffee. I recommended words for three different signs: *Private Property, Aircraft Use This Road, Aircraft Have Right-of-Way and Use Extreme Caution.* Cal said the whole effort was a waste of time since pilots already knew to watch for other aircraft and children.

What!!!

After I recovered, I explained, several times, that the signs were not primarily for *pilots*, they were mainly for *visitors* in cars. Furthermore, the signs would have the dual purpose of warning drivers to be alert while also looking great in court should an incident occur, and we get sued.

"Well, now you are just playing attorney," Cal said. "Why do you want to keep outside people from ever coming in here to visit residents?" I am sure the color drained from my face.

"Is that what you just heard me say, that I want to keep visitors out?"

"Yes."

Now I was truly puzzled. The words I had spoken were not at all the same words Cal had heard in his head. We were at an impasse, and I was not sure what to do.

The room grew completely silent.

Cal made the decision for me when he blurted out "Do whatever you want!", stood up and left.

I bought the custom signs we needed and installed them myself along our streets. Our HOA lawyer commended us on "getting it right" on our signs' wording, for excellent liability protection. I publicly thanked Cal for being on the two-person committee with me and helping choose the words. He knew he had not helped at all but said nothing and basked in the compliments. That was my second warning that Cal had a very different mind.

I had never run into a person whose brain completely changed another person's words enroute to his memory cells. There may have been even more going on with Cal psychologically — he displayed other odd behavior in the community later on.

Lesson Learned: Odd behavior in one area may indicate an odd personality that will eventually cause odd behavior in other areas. Be vigilant with people who are odd in any area. Some idiosyncrasies just come along with really intelligent people but if they cross over into sociopathic behavior, you now have a major problem. (*Rule 21*). Cal was certainly a porcupine. His behavior—heck, his entire being—was prickly. This experience also showed me that it's possible for one person's words to be completely and honestly misconstrued by another. Watch for this phenomenon in your interactions with others and be *curious* when it happens, not *judgmental*. Take the time to determine the cause; sometimes it may be more psychological than mean-spirited.

Therefore:

> ➢ Choose your words carefully. Strive for clarity, then for the correct tone and desired impact.

> ➢ Practice saying things as clearly and concisely as humanly possible, while achieving absolute understanding between the parties.

> ➢ Resist saying or writing things to intentionally hurt other people. You can create enemies for life. (Confession: I have a hard time shrugging off other people's personal attacks on me. My skin is "thicker" than it once was but even now, in my senior years, I continue to thicken my skin.)

> ➢ Develop a large, working vocabulary which is essential to effective communication. Reading extensively and writing frequently are the best ways to build a vocabulary.

> ➢ Listen actively to what others say. Strive to hear what is actually said, not what you expect to hear. Confirm it by restating a compressed version of what you think you heard.

> ➢ Beware of people who twist your words, inadvertently or (especially) intentionally.

Rule 16. Pass the Baton, Learn the Lingo

Rule 17. Motivations Move Mountains

Rule 18. Wearing the Cape is Tempting

Rule 19. Sometimes You Must Kill A Few Puppies

Rule 20. Do not Bayonet Your Own Wounded

Rule 21. Do not Push a Porcupine

Rule 16. Pass the Baton, Learn the Lingo

> Observation: Each generation has at least two responsibilities to the nation: 1) to learn from older generations and 2) to teach younger generations. This process has been broken.

Every young generation entering the workforce needs to learn everything possible from the older workers, the people with the most experience doing that work. The epitome of this principle is the time-tested apprenticeship programs in use throughout societies everywhere. Mike Rowe, host of the Dirty Jobs™ TV series, is actively promoting American apprenticeship programs for 19 skilled trades, with scholarships, placement programs, etc.[14]

Both parties, the teacher and the student, must cooperate to make this work: time must be spent together passing on knowledge, tips, techniques and processes; discussions must occur, with questions and answer sessions; and the language of that profession and of the workplace in general must be passed from older workers to younger ones.

I always tell young people I am coaching and mentoring, "Listen to me and learn from my experience. You do not have time in your career to personally make all the mistakes I have made. And you might not survive them."

Younger generations want coaches more than bosses. As a result, increasingly over the past decade, supervisors have been serving more as mentors than as supervisors. But something terrible happened in 2021-2022: COVID lockdowns and social distancing rules drove most people out of their physical offices and into virtual offices in their homes. From an inter-generational, knowledge transfer standpoint, the effects have been harmful.

- Young people just starting their careers and new to their industry were deprived of close working relationships with more senior, experienced workers. They did not get to witness an entire generation of Baby Boomers for whom punctuality mattered and a strong work ethic was a measure of honor, maturity and willingness to provide for a family.

- Older people, many of them nearing retirement, were stifled in their ability to pass on a full measure of tips, methods, techniques, problem solving skills or language. One estimate is that 10,000 Americans reach

---

14 The MikeRoweWorks Foundation can be found at https://mikeroweworks.org/about/

the age of 65 each year! Many of those people retire at that point, without fully passing on their expertise to the youngest generations coming behind them.

I see in my newsfeeds lots of examples of senior people giving back to their communities and their society, but we need more. We need more still-working seniors, especially business owners and operators willing to coach young entrepreneurs about the challenges of starting a business and proven techniques for growing it. I and four of my fellow business founders taught business start-up basics to military people leaving government service as part of the Transition Assistance Program (TAP) at US bases in England, Germany, Italy and Kuwait. We were "roving professors" for a Syracuse University project hosted by the Institute for Veterans and Military Families called Boots-to-Business. Funded by the US Veterans Administration, this program gave separating US soldiers, sailors, airmen and marines a 2-day crash course in selecting, launching and operating a small business. We need dozens more of these education and training programs, and not just for soon-to-be-former-military people—for everyone.

Regardless of your age or experience, you can help: **Seniors** please take the time to teach. **Young people** seeking experience in the trades or in opening and operating a business, please make your need for the training known to your congressperson, senators, governors and mayors.

Aside from the boost to the real engine of the American economy (small business), the mixing of generations that will result from these business coaching and mentoring sessions will have another benefit: the resulting discussions will help repair that 2020-2022 failure of workplace language-transfer induced by the COVID lockdowns. Our youngest and oldest generations are unable to engage in meaningful communication. In part, this is due to the division caused by Identity Politics where entire groups of people are labeled and denigrated, often based on a single attribute such as age, political affiliation, neighborhood, immigration status, etc. But there may be more than simple tribalism at work with this cancer of cultural *divisions*.

Caution: *Divide and conquer* is not just a historical phrase. This technique is quite common within emergent communist/fascist insurgencies worldwide. Any society can be fragmented by pitting subgroups against each other by the government, "news" organizations, academic institutions and politicians. Then those fragments can be controlled by party operatives, devious politicians and judges, excessive taxation and a willing, compliant media. The result is the death of a culture, the loss of a national identity. In the USA, we have all those entities at work, busily dividing Americans into almost-warring factions.

We must stop that process in America by remembering we are a Republic—one, unique Nation of free people. And in the workplace, we must stop thinking of ourselves as one *generation* or another of people, nor of one (take your choice of noun)—race, color, socio-economic group, and so on. We must not identify first as liberals or conservatives, pro-lifers or pro-woman's choicer, white or non-white, old or young.

Instead, we must first think of ourselves as American citizens and then as *members of one or more professions*: engineers, business developers, project managers, business start-up leaders, IT professionals, hospitality specialists, etc.—regardless of your age or generation. And we must renew our dedication to roll up our sleeves and work with all the other generations and mixes of various people who happen to be in that profession. This includes American citizens and all other reasonable, fair-minded, freedom-loving citizens of the world.

> *Over the last half century, numerous forces from both above and below have conspired to undermine the value we place in the idea of citizenship and our vigilance in protecting it. To be self-governing, citizens must be economically autonomous but the evisceration of the middle class and the rise of inequality have made many Americans dependent on the federal government. . . . A vastly expanded unelected bureaucracy has overwhelmed the power of elected officials thereby destroying the sovereign power of the citizen.*
>
> *—Dr. Victor Davis Hanson[15]*

Communication begins with language. In addition to books like this one, we are doing our part to help both generational extremes, the oldest and the youngest, bridge the language gap. Studies have shown that some young professionals' lack of familiarity with workplace vocabulary is hurting their careers. See section What Next? for one solution.

---

[15] Victor Davis Hanson, "The Dying Citizen" (New York: Basic Books, 2021), hardcover book jacket

Therefore:

➤ Act as the catalyst in your organization, large or small, government or industry, for initiating a knowledge transfer (KT) project. Good grief, you are reading a book about how to initiate, resource, charter, staff, execute, lead, deliver and close out a project! So "cut your teeth" on a KT project! Find other people who will support the KT effort and get them involved too. Yep, this is probably a crappy little job, and you will be doing it in addition to your other work. If you doubt the power of a task like this, or the excellent visibility you will get with your leadership, don't. This is rocket fuel for a career.

➤ Refuse to fall into the easy trap of lazily putting people into categories in your mind, so you no longer must treat people as individuals. Again, be curious about human behavior, not judgmental.

➤ Change the dangerous trajectory of politics by refusing to accept skewed stories on news feeds, with their spin and bias. Instead, watch and listen to multiple, opposing news sources and use your critical thinking skills to test the information being fed to us all. Demand unbiased, fact-based news sources and when you think you have found one, test it against other sources for accuracy and truth. If it passes the test, support that source financially.

➤ Decide what society you want to hand over to the next generation and work to make that happen.

Rule 17. Motivations Move Mountains

> Observation: Understanding the motivations of customers, bosses and colleagues is essential to keeping a project low-drama and on track. But even that does not guarantee your team a success or even a future on the program.

Things may not always work out the way you want them to. When they don't, that does not make you a "victim" or give you the right to stomp your feet, scream at people, or initiate lawsuits. Stuff just happens.

Whenever you are considering a new endeavor, figure out who has what motivations. (*Rules 2 and 17*) What is the organization trying to do with the project or decision? Make a large profit? Support an ongoing research and development effort or contribute a key capability to some other contract? Show senior leaders that we are attempting to do something impossible? Rotate managers through several jobs to give them cross-company exposure? Keep the company's name visible in the industry? Any of these and more are possible.

The answer will drive how you manage the project. I have experienced all those reasons and more. Always ask the magic question, "What are we trying to do with this project?" This will tell you what success looks like.

Understand the Boss's Motivation

In addition to holding back a program's rationale unless prodded, some bosses hold back resources too, as a way to ensure project leaders do not burn through the funding too quickly. Their motivation is likely to be financial — not running short of funds before key milestones are reached or deliverables are completed.

Bosses are sometimes in a hurry to get projects launched and quick to assign projects to managers, but sometimes less eager to ensure each has all the long-term resources to do the work and the authority to make key decisions. These bosses are also the most likely to omit the important *Project Charter* which lays out for the team the *what*, *why* and *how* of a project. Sometimes, as project manager, you are justified in hesitating to immediately take on every problem offered by the project team or even by your management, until you understand the motivations.

Know What Motivates Yourself and Others

As managers and leaders, you will on occasion be surprised by comments that your people or customers make and questions they ask. Supervisors may confront you with probing questions related to why you took an action or why you made a decision. Customers may ask you similar questions. Employees may ask why you assigned them a certain task, or why they did not get a promotion. These confrontational discussions can turn nasty.

We will get to the possible motivations of other people shortly. First, it's important that you think about, and try to understand, the motivation behind your own actions that caused others to question you before you answer those questions. Train yourself to think first in terms of resolving conflict and establishing a collaborative relationship. (*Rule 20*) Get past those Positions to the underlying Interests! (*Rule 6*). Perhaps the sharp question posed by an employee is warranted—*seek first to understand, then to be understood* is not just a catchy phrase. Did your behavior slip into a little selfishness? Did you launch a directive without thinking through all the possibilities, via the What-If exercise explained elsewhere in this book?

When someone makes a comment that is politically motivated, confrontational or precipitated by apparent anger, recognize you may be dealing with a prickly, porcupine-person. Do not give in to your own human urge to fight or flee. Just freeze. Do nothing.

Simply pause for 4-5 seconds before you say anything at all. You are buying time to think, to choose words to defuse the situation, not to inflame it. More importantly, you are avoiding saying the first thing that comes to mind which has been statistically and verifiably proven to be almost always wrong! Finally, you are encouraging the speaker to explain themselves, to share why they feel that way. You are seeking to understand their motivations. You do this, after your pause, by calmly asking a variation of:

- Why would you ask me that?
- Why would you say that?

And then wait for a reply.

If the other person now explains the reason they asked you that question or made that comment (perhaps even their motivation), then excellent! You can discuss the situation. You will have gotten more information about their motivation, why they said or asked what they did. And you will have gained some time to think. They may say, "Just joking! I wanted to see your reaction.

Ha ha." If so, wouldn't you be glad you did not react angrily yourself and make the situation worse?

They may give a non-response such as "YOU know why I said that!" You pause again and reply, "I am just really surprised to hear you say that." And regardless of what happens after this, you have done five things, all of them good:

1. Bought time to think and to formulate questions of your own.

2. Asked for further clarification of the initial confrontational statement/accusation made against you. It may have been based on completely inaccurate information.

3. Showed calmness, a refusal to lose your temper.

4. Stayed professional, in word and demeanor.

5. Demonstrated that your interest is maintaining a good relationship with that person and collaboratively solving issues, not just trying to win an argument.

If you can easily and quickly correct some honest misunderstanding or some misconception the other person has, do it, right then and there. If it's a significant issue, offer to discuss a resolution in person, later, and not on the phone or virtually unless you are geographically separated and unlikely to be able to meet face-to-face. Why? Again, this buys you time to research the problem, to think through key issues and to ask confidants for their opinions and recommendations. And difficult conversations are always easier to have in-person, where you can read the other person's body language and where your genuineness and honesty can shine through.

Other's Motivations Can Make or Break Your Project

You must have the best possible people on your project, those motivated by the same things as you. This collaborative group mindset is typically more important than having enough money to complete the effort because properly motivated staff who are resourceful and well-connected can often help find additional funding. Ensure everyone shares your motivations.

Project staffing levels are usually budget constrained. To afford the people you need, do not pay for people you do not need. Some people are motivated by things other than the success of your project and these people can be a burden. One particular breed of porcupine-people (*Rule 21*) cannot or will not be taught new, collaborative behaviors and will require massive amounts of handholding. They may have hidden agendas or have selfish motivations that run counter to the project's best interests. Those prickly people need a position outside your project. Find other places for them to work—within your organization if you must, or in a different organization altogether (even better).

Others with Hidden Motivations May Decide When You Are Finished

There are simply no guarantees that a project will "succeed" in the way you forecast. Often, the client's motivations and long-term plans may not include you or your team.

Example 1. I once helped explore the feasibility of a sensor to support counter-narcotics efforts. The research assessed whether a device being used by drug cartels in the jungle could be detected by an airborne sensor from the device's radio frequency (RF) emissions. Our team calculated the signal-to-noise ratio as being exploitable with the right receiver-processor even through an RF-absorbing/scattering, triple-canopy jungle.

We fabricated a proof-of-concept detection system and field-tested it in Virginia. We had hopes of putting the sensor systems into production, where some real money could be made. All test and evaluation criteria/ gates were met. We were told it transitioned to an airborne prototype that was successfully flown in the operational environment.

Then, poof!

The corporate client paid us and thanked us, and the effort disappeared. That was it. We were not offered work in optimizing the design or any other follow-on activity. The customer already knew exactly which firm he wanted to build those production systems, and it was not us (hidden motivations). We did not claim intellectual property rights, or demand a position on the production team, or insist on royalties. Our little team was not a "victim"; we were simply not the customer's first choice for the next phase. The program took on a new life and moved on. As did we. But I like to think that, for a few years, we helped cause drug lords in central and south America some major problems.

Example 2. I was project manager for an R&D effort to develop a capability to detect hard-to-find battlefield emitters, Project ELVIS. I worked for months lining up US Army, Navy and Air Force offices to support us with an AH-64D Apache helicopter, an F-18 Hornet and an F-16 Viper. I got the helicopter formally committed by the Army in Huntsville but the Navy's PMA-265 (F-18) office said they would only commit if the Air Force provided an F-16 for the project. Try as I might, I could never convince the Air Force's

Air Combat Command (ACC) to commit the F-16 aircraft to the project. Politics! So the entire effort, six months of my life, was mostly wasted.

But I did not allow myself to think of my team as "victims." I had developed a slightly thicker skin many years earlier. It has paid off for me many times as I faced difficulties. I have since learned how to end-run obstructionist Iron Majors like the one at ACC who killed project ELVIS. If I were leading a similar effort now, I would involve the Air National Guard which is usually easier to work with than active duty USAF units. Hold your emails please. I have served with both communities and love them both. But the latter has more red tape.

Example 3. As manager of an applied R&D team at a major corporation, I inherited a license agreement for $5 million with a UK company to use a certain technology. My company should never have entered into this agreement, but it did, and I now owned it. I asked what my leadership's expectations were for the success of the agreement. They said "make money with it if you can, but don't let it go to court, where several others like it have already ended up!" I busted my @$$ trying to sell products worldwide, using the technology we had licensed, but we couldn't even give the stuff away. While we did manage to get some work with a derivative product, the sales results were disappointing enough to the UK government that I was "invited" to London to explain our company's actions at Whitehall, their Pentagon. In the end, we headed to court, but my bosses managed to settle everything before an expensive arbitration.

I failed to manage that relationship to a successful conclusion with the Brits. And, if you are trying hard enough, you will fail at a few things too. Just do not fall into the *I failed, therefore I'm a failure, and I'm a victim* syndrome. Some people fail at things often enough that they mentally label themselves failures. To protect their ego, they then try to blame their misfortunes entirely on other people or on outside events beyond their control, which then makes them a victim. You cannot allow yourself to think of yourself as a failure or a victim, nor can you allow your employees to even begin to think of themselves as victims.

A Cautionary Note on Victimhood

Victim status is a mindset that will destroy your career and your personal life. Bad things happen to everyone. You must make your own way in this world, and there will be occasional brushes with bad people, unfair situations, projects that fall apart, porcupine people, terrible companies and agencies, and personal defeats. As the US Marine Corps says, "Improvise and Overcome!" Roll with the punches and come back fighting. People who accept the title of victim may find solace in the sympathy they get from others. It helps them feel better about themselves ("wow, it wasn't my fault at all!") and they begin to look at every interaction as an opportunity to further their victimhood. They graduate from being offended at even innocent actions by other people, actions they find objectionable for any reason, to being the victim of *language* used by other people.

If you find any of your team members "walking around spring-loaded in the pissed-off position" as an old Sergeant once described to me, have a serious chat with them. They have become porcupines! Tell them what they are doing and the effect they are having on others. Instead of deploying quills, develop thick skin.

Therefore:

➤ Refuse to cooperate in being set-up to fail. Be slow to commit, and loath to disappoint. Think through complex issues before answering every question posed to you by management, employees or clients. Recognize that some of the questions may be traps.

➤ Develop thick skin. Refuse to think of yourself as a victim.

➤ Refuse to give other people space in your head, because it distracts, slows your ability to recover, and is wildly contagious. (*Rule 8*)

➤ Remember you are human, especially when you fail. Learn from failures by talking to people, especially to a few real friends, those who will listen and be honest, those who will tell you what they really think. These are your "truth tellers".

➤ Understand that close friends and kindred spirits can be a great comfort when you need an attitude adjustment. Learn not to gripe against the event or person who caused failure. Surround yourself with calm, pleasant people.

➤ Cut yourself some slack as you learn new skills!

➤ Don't be a porcupine! Friends don't let friends become porcupines either!

Rule 18. Wearing the Cape is Tempting

> Observation: When we are new to a team, we want to prove ourselves.

Everyone wants to be a superhero. But in donning the cape rashly, you may over-promise and fail. Do not let your ego lead you down this trail. Guard against the tendency to take on more than the available resources or schedule will allow.

You will need to be alert to the temptation of a hasty start throughout your career, even when you have been in an organization for many years. The greatest danger is, counterintuitively, when offered an especially attractive job: one you are dying to tackle. Why is this? Unattractive assignments cause us to pause and think about what could go wrong. A glittering job, however, short-circuits our natural tendency to consider the offer objectively. A tempting, sparkling project dangled before our eyes blinds us to the realities of what the project entails. We just want to put on our cape and leap tall buildings!

But there is a simple way to avoid this problem when an extremely attractive project comes your way. Use a checklist that you develop and tailor for all your project start-ups. That way, no steps are inadvertently omitted.

How do we deal with demanding customers?

When a customer demands fast work at some ridiculously low price, go to your desk and stare intently at a sign you will have constructed there that reads:

Schedule or Price: Customers can pick ONE.

These are the priorities that you, our would-be superhero project leader, will consider given a task. How much time can be allocated and what funding is necessary to do an excellent job? You will find that these priorities are like rubber bands; they pull each other.

So now we ask, what is the customer's perspective on this? Before buying into a project, you will let the customer specify their most important priority: fast or slow, expensive or cheap. Everyone wants high quality no matter what they are willing to pay or how quickly they expect to receive their product.

High quality should always be a given because you are a would-be superhero with a reputation to build.

Example 1. A customer asks your team to perform a study at a moderate cost. The customer's top priority is budget. You negotiate a realistic schedule knowing it will take longer to complete a high-quality study on a small budget.

Example 2. A customer asks your team to perform a study in half the amount of time it typically takes. This customer has prioritized the schedule. You negotiate a higher fee than usual because you know you need to gather extra resources to get this done in record time.

Example 3. A customer asks you to conduct a study in a short amount of time, with a low budget. The customer has taken rein of both priorities: schedule and budget. They assume you will willingly lower the quality of your work. But you won't. You walk away. The customer never gets to force you to opt for poor quality, because your name is on that product. Never let a customer box you into a corner where you must do poor quality work. Period.

When you demonstrate the ability to consistently, correctly balance the two basic priorities, schedule and price, while maintaining high quality, you are on your way to becoming a credible super-hero project leader!

Therefore:

➤ **Do not be hasty when jumping into a job that will make you a superhero. Slow down and think before you put that cape on! Look, twice, before you leap!**

➤ **Force yourself to consider what planning and resources are needed before you start a project.**

➤ **Remember: "Schedule or Price: Customers Can Pick One."**

➤ **Keep the high quality of your work non-negotiable; it should always be something that makes you proud.**

Rule 19. Sometimes You Must Kill A Few Puppies

> Observation: Projects can take on a life of their own (and sometimes a project's life should end early).

It's easy for people who work hard on a project to become emotionally attached. However, projects are not living things, no matter how enamored contributors become of them. If a project's viability drops due to loss of funding, mediocre performance of technologies, loss of key talent, or other major problems, then it should be reviewed for termination. It should be cancelled or at least restructured. Most projects like this will have gathered an entourage of followers and advocates who will clamor loudly that the project shall live on! Fighting these people can be exhausting, but it must be done.

Project Managers and team leaders must develop clear and objective gates, milestones and off-ramps. Know when to abort a failing project. The only thing worse than having initially funded a shaky project is spending even more money on it and then it fails! To ensure careers are not impacted when a project must be abandoned, consider giving awards for "Outstanding Risk Mitigation" (aka "failure") for having reduced the risk to the company.

My daughter, Molly, is in the media business where video production staff often discard video sections to meet a firm timeline. Creative staffers may have worked many long and hard hours to record, re-record, sort and edit each of those segments. Those artists love those products like you love a puppy! So experts in that business refer to the often-excruciating task of discarding favorite video segments as "being as painful as killing puppies."

Example 1. In a microcosm, I can attest to the pain of this process; writing and rewriting this book was painful. Typically, after spending hours composing a meaty section I thought would be interesting to my readers, I would be told by one of my reviewers or by my editor, "Not on-topic. Delete this section entirely." That was not as traumatic as killing an actual puppy but I hated to see all that work wasted. I admit this book is more readable because of it. (Heads up, all those trimmings will reappear in future books!)

Example 2. Years ago, when I moved from C3I Systems at Westinghouse Defense into Advanced Systems for airborne fire control with some amazing engineers, I was assigned a crappy little job (*Rule 4*) to assemble a collection of advanced technology stories concerning future directions in radar processing, digital processing, RF apertures, electro-optical apertures, signature reduction, electronic warfare techniques, and advanced packaging of electronics. I was given two months. The American Institute of Aeronautics and Astronautics (AIAA) sponsored this. We were to provide a non-proprietary, unclassified version to them.

In assembling this information, I talked with dozens of Westinghouse's brightest engineers and I learned, first-hand, where the trends were headed on topics such as gallium arsenide, active electronically scanned arrays (AESAs), and exotic materials. That knowledge, while not deep, broadened my technical horizons. Those conversations led to friendships with amazing people who were the nation's thought leaders in their fields. Doing that "crappy little job" resulted in friendships that I would benefit from for decades at Westinghouse and then afterward when we were bought by Northrop Grumman.[16]

At the culmination of the project, I flew out to a California air-framer's location to help with a briefing of our report. I had about four hours' worth of carefully built, well-researched slides assembled by our company's engineers. Yet when I arrived, I discovered we were only allotted two hours. Yep, I had to kill a lot of "puppies" — more than half of my slides — on the spot.

Example 3: *An exception to this rule*: Some projects are too important to be dismantled or to have parts discarded, for any reason. For these, you either do them completely or not at all. As mentioned elsewhere in this book, Viking chieftains, upon arriving on the shore of a new country they intended to settle, would often empty, then burn their boats! This was an unmistakable message to the crew, "We are here to stay, boys. Make it work." The core business of the Vikings was to invade and settle. They could not go back. Burning the boats gave the men motivation to fight to the death! One such project for me turned out to be the controller training program in Germany discussed elsewhere in this book. When I arrived in Germany and saw how impossible the task would be, I considered abandoning the project at its inception. I am glad I didn't. I realized that the mission to train US combat air crews was more important than my concerns. I decided I would see it through and do what I could to build the program. Once I started, I was committed. There were no decision points where I would consider exiting the project. I would make it happen "come hell or high water" as we say in West Virginia!

---

[16] In good organizations, military and civilian, you will often make friends for life. I still have lunch with many of those fine, former-Westinghouse Defense people every month here in the Baltimore area.

Caution: Do not plan to use project off-ramps (kill puppies) for any process or series of activities that cannot be stopped after it passes a tipping point. Allowed to progress long enough, some processes reach a point-of-no-return. Some can even change, becoming malignant and beginning to consume the host. The "puppy" becomes a fully-grown wolf and is no longer controllable. Three notable examples of *one-time-and-you-are-done* dangers include: crystal meth—many people are deeply addicted after the first use; fentanyl—few people dabble with fentanyl because enough exposure, even the first time, maybe with a particle the size of a grain of sand, can kill you; and some political constructs (governments).

My macro-example of things we do not trifle with is a freedom-extinguishing, politico-economic situation where a large, all-powerful central government controls most of the "means of production", the companies— factories, transportation, harbors, hotels, etc. For decades in Russia, that controlling entity has been powerful oligarchs. Readers of this book will see this discussed on news feeds. These are criminal networks with a central figurehead and controlled by the government, who own/control all industry. Sometimes called *corporatocracies*, examples abound worldwide, and some argue the unholy triad of US intelligence agencies, hi tech/social media firms in Silicon Valley (especially *Artificial Intelligence*), and the mainstream media, are starting to make the US look like a *corporatocracy*! (See *Rule 23*.)

More widely seen is the arrangement where a large, all-powerful central government openly controls all industry, without the middle-men oligarchs. These places—Cuba, Russia, China, North Korea, Myanmar and others— have no free enterprise system. Instead, a monolithic, monstrous central hive of self-installed bureaucrats oversees layer upon layer of restrictions and government approval mazes.

The centrally-controlled nations mentioned above are extremely restrictive: Unless you are politically or financially well-connected (already powerful and rich), you will not be permitted to start, "buy" or operate a business of any kind. And even then, you will operate when, where and how the *government* tells you to operate. And most, maybe all, of your profits go back to your masters, not to you, your family or employees.

No independent *middle class* can survive in those countries. A thriving, vibrant middle class (where most of the readers of this book fit) is the engine of new business formation in any country. Individual entrepreneurs spring up, get an idea for a business to serve an unmet (or underserved) need in the marketplace, risk their own money and launch their business ventures. An unforgiving, uncontrolled free market, unfettered by government meddling or control, then decides what products and services survive versus those that get modified, merged or dissolved.

I have been describing the Borg-like[17] vision being offered by a radical cabal of public and private entities. They push across a wide front of news feeds, academic institutions, and political movements and their approaches have some common refrains:

1. More control of your life by a huge and growing central government (insurance, medical care, retirement plans, schools, unions, federal judicial system, larger Supreme Court, etc.)

2. Fewer detached family homes and more "planned", high-occupancy housing units.

3. Less focus on the importance of the family unit with two parents in the home

4. In the US, less power in the hands of the individual states

The expressed goal is noble: a socialist utopia where everyone's needs are met, and everyone is cared for from cradle to grave. But it has never worked, at any of the many places it has been tried, starting with the Pilgrims at Plymouth Rock! They initially made the tasks of growing food, maintaining shelter, etc. shared responsibilities. They soon found that a few industrious people were working themselves to death trying to support freeloaders and slackers. They learned *if something is everyone's job, then no one will do it.* So, they reorganized into plots of land divided up among the residents. That arrangement worked well—people worked hard to care for their own land and possessions and the resulting harvests provided enough food to share with each other and their native American neighbors, not the other way around as is portrayed in many history books.

Remember the adage from President Gerald Ford, "A government big enough to give you everything you want is a government big enough to take from you everything you have." Dr. Mark Levin says it best, regarding the impracticality of a utopia:

> *Clearly, utopianism is incompatible with constitutionalism. Utopianism requires power to be concentrated in a central authority with maximum latitude to transform and control. Oppositely, a constitution establishes parameters that define the*

---

17 Star Trek fans will recognize the hive-like Borg as a race of half-human, half-AI bot creatures bent on assimilating every other race in the universe. Borgs were centrally controlled and ruthless.

form and the limits of government. . . . The constitution enshrines a governing framework intended to ensure the longevity of the existing society and stifle the potential for tyranny. [18]

I am the Last of My Kind

It will come as no surprise to the historically savvy reader that the above four goals are also essential planks of the Marxist-Leninist-Maoist communist/ socialist platform worldwide. Now, before your eyes glaze over and you think "political rant approaching, please no", hear this: I have seen it! I have seen communism at work!

Wars have been fought to defeat fascist and communist maniacs from Borg-style takeovers of big swathes of the planet. My generation of Baby Boomers is the last group of still-working Americans to have talked first-hand with WWll survivors. I have met WWll-era Germans and Americans, civilians and soldiers who told me about the slow, steady march of Naziism in Germany.

I served in uniform during the Cold War, so I have seen first-hand the effects of central control essential to communism and socialism. Once my cohorts and I die, lessons learned and stories can only come from history books and YouTube videos. You will not have first or second-hand accounts from people like me, who personally saw and heard incredible things.

---

[18] Mark Levin, "Ameritopia – The Unmaking of America" (New York: Threshold Editions, 2012)

In getting my arms around my own worldview and forming my moral code, I realized that serving as a US Air Force officer during the Cold War also gave me an interesting perspective. I have walked the streets of communist/ socialist East Germany and Berlin, and looked across the Iron Curtain into the abyss — the Marxist-communist Soviet regime that Stalin imposed on millions of entrapped people at the end of World War ll. I have witnessed the amazing differences in quality of life for people in formerly communist East Germany, before and after the fall of the Berlin Wall.

I have lectured for the Cold War Museum in Vent Hill, Virginia, and talked with people who witnessed unspeakable horrors in communist nations. I have worked with people in countries that were former communist Warsaw Pact nations (Slovenia, Croatia, Serbia, Bosnia Herzegovina and Hungary) but which now are at least semi-democracies.

I have met and talked with defectors including a Czech Air Force General, a pilot, who one day, gave up everything to flee to the freedom of the West. I asked him why he chose that particular day to defect. He explained that the ground crew had mistakenly filled his fighter's tanks that morning! On his pre-flight, walk-around inspection, when he saw that his fuel tanks were full, he knew he would have enough fuel to make it to a West German airfield someplace, so he jumped in the MiG jet and left. Headquarters scrambled other MiGs to intercept him but as he listened to his pursuers calling him repeatedly on the aircraft's radio, he made it across the border before they could reach him.

That pilot left all his family and relatives behind. When I talked with him several years later, he said the ground crewman who mistakenly filled those fuel tanks was probably executed. The US did get the General's wife and children out several years after that.

For me, communism/Marxism/socialism is not some abstract concept that can be experimented with in the US. For almost every person you meet who was born after about 1958, the stark differences between free-market societies and socialist/communist regimes are learned from a book.

I am slightly older and **I was there**.

Communism/Marxism/socialism is a social malignancy. The life-lessons I learned, watching it spread like a cancer through various nations, shaped my own worldview and formed some of the *Rules* — and cautions — in this book. It inexplicably remains a threat to both the Republic we have here in the USA, and the US Constitution I am still sworn to protect. Socialism (in addition to communism) is a militant, political quagmire that no nation can afford to dabble with. Once a tipping point is reached in the central control of a nation's economy, military and justice systems (or the control of any TWO of those), there is no turning back; no "off-ramps" designed-in earlier will function. In this case, the puppy *has* become a young wolf and the host society will be eaten.

Ask the people in China, North Korea or Cuba what they have seen and experienced. Oh, that's right, you cannot ask them. All news and social media there are closely monitored and controlled. And if you did somehow ask them, they could not answer you for fear of imprisonment or worse.

Therefore:

> ➢ Set decision points for your projects that serve as off-ramps where you can cut your losses if certain things do not happen.

> ➢ Kill non-critical projects (aka puppies) as soon as it becomes apparent that they have become untenable, irrelevant or undesirably redundant.

> ➢ Encourage Project Managers to involve higher management in go/no-go decisions, to help pick the best strategic times to terminate, restructure, or transfer a project that is in trouble.

> ➢ Reward managers and leaders who recognize a failing program and terminate it before it negatively impacts the company. Projects terminated for reasonable causes (but not gross mismanagement) are good candidates.

> ➢ Use good judgement to determine when it's prudent to finish a tough job that you have started, even though it has proven to be much harder than you anticipated. Do this especially when other people are counting on you to see it through.

> ➢ Save some puppies, those that are crucial to the survival of the organization. If they are considered sacrosanct, they may be worth all the resources poured into them.

> ➢ Realize that the American, constitutionally based, representative republic we have now is fundamentally incompatible with socialism or communism. Period.

➤ Get involved! Fixing America's projects and programs will be of no value if we lose the Republic. So, you readers in western-style democracies, republics and similar cultures around the world, please get involved politically and stop the seemingly inexorable march toward oligarchies, dictatorships, crony-capitalism and central federal control. In the USA, we must get back to an enlightened federal republic, with its free market and State's rights, just as our Founding Fathers intended. That will save you, our middle class. Here in America, that reversal begins with curtailing the near-constant power grabs by zealous government denizens in Washington DC.

➤ Vote and vote carefully. Otherwise, you will have wasted your money on this leadership and business book. The central government will soon provide the former, so there will be no need for the latter.

➤ Be cautious about allowing artificial intelligence to proliferate across your non-military governmental agencies, or even be readily accessible to them via the private sector. See Rule 23 for a further explanation of this risk.

Rule 20. Do Not Bayonet Your Own Wounded After the Battle

> Observation: We can only learn from past mistakes if we acknowledge and dissect them for lessons learned.

As a professional in any organization, regardless of your experience level, you will attend occasional lessons-learned sessions after projects, proposals, contracts or other milestone events. Corporate Business Development people often host post-proposal and post-capture sessions and generate After-Action Reports or AARs, to find and socialize ways to improve their processes. I have attended hundreds of these. The best AAR sessions occurred when everyone, senior leadership included, did what we also did in the Air Force after each air-to-air training mission: we "took our rank off" and spoke as tactician to tactician, operator-to-operator. Open, honest discussions uncovered things we each could have done better, mistakes that we made and processes that needed to be changed.

Unfortunately, I have seldom found that Air Force level of honest discussion in the corporate world. Instead, I have seen that many senior people are psychologically unable to participate as equals with workers; they cannot "remove their rank" and accept criticism from the employees. Their egos prevent them from effectively participating in postmortem sessions. They tend to criticize people with their comments and questions during AARs. They rehash old wounds, relive perceived slights and belittle other people's decisions. When anyone's decisions or actions disagree with how they (the managers) would have acted, those are cases of "poor judgement". In short, these managers bayonet their own wounded.

Example 1. Years ago, I witnessed senior corporate BD people stifling comments and positive suggestions from our employees during lessons-learned sessions. They never stepped up and accepted responsibility for their own mistakes and that set a bad example. I stopped inviting those supervisors to the sessions. Sadly, rather than learn a lesson themselves, once they were no longer invited, they became even more disconnected, further eroding the level of trust across the organization.

As a Project Manager or team leader, after every major activity that has a clearly defined endpoint, force everyone involved to say, in writing, at least one thing that could have been done better. Then at a group gathering (virtual or in-person), mention everyone on the team, by name, and say what that person did to help. Thank them individually, in public. Also encourage them to say what they could have done better on the recently ended job. This is difficult for many people to do but essential.

As the SEAL Mark Owen said, "The hardest thing to do is honestly communicate with people, especially when you may be at fault ... The thing to remember is that communication and the lessons learned from the AAR are only put in place to make the team better."[19]

Example 2. I observed a senior BD Capture Manager share with his team several actions he had taken during a project, actions that he thought he and others could improve upon in the future. Later I heard that his supervisor used the same lessons-learned comments against that Capture Manager in an unrelated legal action. That was the ultimate breach of trust and demonstrated self-serving betrayal. I never worked with that firm again.

Therefore:

> ➢ **Do a friendly, collaborative post-mortem AAR after every job. Keep the atmosphere non-confrontational. Make sure every participant talks about what they, personally, could have done differently to produce better outcomes.**

> ➢ **Brief everyone in advance as to what will be expected. Be honest and open about your own mistakes and things you could have done better; be gentle in bringing up others' mistakes.**

> ➢ **Avoid using, adversely, anything unflattering that you hear someone say about themselves in AAR sessions.**

> ➢ **Leave the organization if you see leadership using employees' self-appraisals in a punitive way. Find another job. For management to encourage employees to expose their honest mistakes, for the common good, and then to use those in an adverse way, is inexcusable.**

---

[19] Mark Owen and Kevin Mauer "No Hero" (London: Penguin Random House, 2015) pages 139 and 158.

Rule 21.   Do Not Push a Porcupine

Observation: We encounter challenging, prickly projects and people throughout our careers and lives. Learning to deal with them effectively is essential to successful projects and to your healthy mental state.

Challenging projects are increasingly common: staff turnovers, budget shortfalls and aggravating leaders. Many of the *Rules* in this book offer guidance on refusing to launch an impossible project (*Rules* 3 and 18) and how to nudge one back onto the tracks if it has run off the rails. The key is to engage the entire project staff in crafting a cure plan to return a project to a successful path. Lead them, do not try to push them. Getting and keeping staff involved in the plan taps into their resources and connections and makes the plan's success their success. People fight hardest for things for which they feel even partial ownership. Make it their plan, not just your plan. And lead them, from the front, just as you would if trying to get a pet porcupine to move in any given direction. You sure would not try to push it!

Leading and dealing with prickly people is also a challenge. The lead-from-the-front approach works best here as well. Lead by example, make the project about the project, not about you. Find ways to get everyone on the team fully engaged: no "quiet quitting." There is one major exception to the involve-everybody approach: sociopaths. Like porcupines, sociopaths seem non-threatening at first glance. If a porcupine decides you are a threat, however, look out! It will attempt to get alongside you in just the right position so that with a swing of its tail you will suddenly understand why no one messes with a porcupine! Ask any dog that tangles with one.

Sociopaths are porcupine people on steroids, and they walk among us. They are toxic to an organization and can be lethal to the careers of people they target. They exist everywhere, in all cultures and all professions. They often look completely normal on the outside, but they will suck the life out of you, your team and your project. Dr. Martha Stout,[20] a noted expert in psychotherapy, calls them "people who have no conscience and can do anything at all without feeling guilty." Sociopaths are narcissistic to the point of seriously manipulating and damaging other people for their own purposes, or sometimes for no reason at all, just for "sport." They drive other

---

[20] Dr. Martha Stout's excellent books on sociopaths include "The Sociopath Next Door" by Broadway Books, NY, NY 2005 and "Outsmarting the Sociopath Next Door" by Harmony Books, NY, NY, 2020,

people's careers and lives downward so that they can feel more important about themselves. Dr. Stout and other researchers estimate that one out of every 25 people (4%) in the general public is a sociopath!

Books abound that explain in detail how to recognize sociopaths. The person might be a sociopath if they:

- Insist that something is a certain way, when it clearly is not

- Intentionally harm another person via character assassination and gossip without cause

- Manipulate others unnecessarily

- Hurt animals for pleasure

- Bully other people and enjoy the power

- Lie about you, to your face, without remorse

- Weaponize others against a targeted person

- Tell you one thing and then act in the reverse without explanation or remorse

- Consistently cast themselves as the victim in any disagreement or conflict

Read books dealing with this subject so you can recognize the telltale signs of sociopathic behavior and stay away from those sad, dangerously prickly individuals. Sociopaths are the special case to the "don't allow bullying" counsel in Rules 8 and 9. If you find a sociopathic person, and you can quietly arrange it, see if they can be evaluated by a mental health professional. If that is not feasible or they react violently to the mere suggestion, I would terminate that person's employment. Be certain you have fully documented their behavior and get support from HR and your organization's senior leadership.

If you lack "top cover" support or do not have a well-documented case, at least reassign them to a position where they have minimum ability to manipulate other people. If they do not work for you directly, and you cannot reassign them elsewhere, learn from what you see and enlist the help of other managers.

Example 1. Sociopathic behaviors seldom appear all at once, but some indicators can appear suddenly. In the middle of a briefing I was giving on L-band radar technology to the senior staff at a US company, the president of that company suddenly corrected me by saying that the aircraft I was discussing carried an S-band radar. I explained that the predecessor aircraft did have an S-band radar but that this new one had an L-band radar, and we had gone to a lot of trouble at my former company to pick the best radar band for the multi-mission system. That L-band MESA radar rode atop Boeing 737-700 airframes in a large, dorsal fin—the Australian Air Force E-7 Wedgetail. I had recently been working personally on that radar and he knew it.

I was speechless for a few seconds.

I had never run into a professional so cock-sure of himself, in the presence of a subject matter expert (me) who had a strong, opposite opinion. This was the President and CEO of the company, and my boss! I paused to collect my thoughts. None came to me.

But he was not going to budge and continued to insist, increasingly loudly, that this was an S-band radar. I ignored his "corrections" and continued the briefing. At the coffee break, when I mentioned this guy's bizarre behavior to his staff, they shrugged and one lady said, "Yeah, that's the boss," as if this kind of egoistic, non-technical behavior happened all the time, and that they were OK with it. (*Rule 4*) After seeing some other indicators over the next few months, I decided that this corporate president was a card-carrying sociopath and I spruced up my resume. I later learned that most of the executive staff drew a tight, protective circle around this man. All of them had drunk the Kool-Aid. *Mobbing* came shortly after this, and I soon stopped working with that company. (*Rule 9*)

Example 2. In a homeowner's association (HOA) I belonged to, one particular resident seemed to be a normal person—personable and friendly—until he was elected to the HOA board of directors, at which point a different personality emerged. He became unhinged. He acted as though he never had any real authority in his life and maybe had never seen himself as part of a team. The power of speaking on behalf of a group of people changed him: he took independent actions without involving the rest of the HOA board. Later, we saw other behaviors such as openly lying, verbally attacking HOA members, and building a clique of people he could control. He also painted himself as the victim at every opportunity which clearly identified him as a card-carrying, highly functional sociopath. Had we identified him earlier, we might have been able to minimize the emotional turmoil he caused the neighborhood.

A near cousin to the sociopath is a "virtucrat."[21] "Eventually. . . some of the characteristics of the virtucrat are revealed, chief among them being his belief in his own moral superiority."

> *The virtucrat is certain he has virtue on his side. The virtue being laid claim to is public virtue; it is the virtue that comes from the certainty that one's own opinions are the only correct opinions.[22]*

When their position on a topic is refuted

> *...with logic, facts and statistics, virtucrats will accuse the challenger of being heartless, and therefore, morally inferior. 'You may be correct, but for all the wrong reasons, so I'm a better person than you!' With nothing to sustain their worldviews, virtucrats fabricate their own sense of sanctimonious virtue – an ideology that trumps all earthly reasoning.*
>
> — *Mark Ferbrache*

And the most frustrating, vexing personality I have run into is the combination virtucrat-sociopath. This especially prickly personality type is a topic for another book.

What do you do if you find a sociopath in your midst? First ask, "Can a true sociopath be rehabilitated or change their spots?" No, they cannot. The first

---

[21] "True Value" by Joseph Epstein, The New York Times Magazine, 24 Nov 1985. https://www.nytimes.com/1985/11/24/magazine/true-virtue.html as reported by Mark Ferbrache, The Daily Caller online, 18 Feb 2023, at https://dailycaller.com/2023/02/18/ferbrache-the-rise-of-the-federal-virtuecrats/ The term is spelled both "virtuecrat" and "virtucrat" in the articles.

[22] Ibid

time you see a suspected-sociopathic action, you should politely confront the person about their actions. If the person ceases their toxic behavior, they are probably NOT a sociopath. As Dr. Stout says, "two strikes (not three) and they're out." After being confronted once, a person who continues with disruptive or manipulative behavior is likely to be a sociopath. Do not try to reform them. Get away from them.

If a sociopath singles you out, and puts you in their sights, you have entered a social kill-zone. The sociopath has no sense of proportionality and no feelings of guilt to inhibit them. They are vindictive and capable of severe retribution if you do something against them such as reporting them to a boss or to Human Resources. Your only option is to leave the organization. For the sake of your mental well-being, get out! Find a better work environment.

Can You Identify the Sociopath Among These People? Neither Can We!

Therefore:

➢ Just as you wouldn't mess with an aggravated porcupine even if you were a zoo worker and needed to get a porcupine into a different enclosure, you certainly would not try to push one from behind, would you? So, don't work with or for porcupine-like sociopathic people.

➢ Recognize that sociopaths don't wear signs that say "*I am mentally wrecked and toxic."*

➢ Do not let sociopaths cause you sufficient stress to ruin your health, destroy your life, or even end it if they engage in psychopathic behavior.

➢ Leave the organization if a sociopath has targeted you personally.

➢ Find another position in the organization (quietly) if you detect that your boss is a sociopath, and stay off their "radar."

➢ Make no disparaging remarks about the sociopath. Move on.

Rule 22.   Stay Focused on the Main Thing

Rule 23.   When the AI Bots Get Caught

Rule 24.   Be Short, Be Sweet and Be Gone

Rule 22. Stay Focused on the Main Thing

> Observation: We all want to please our bosses. Yet some bosses put their career interests above those of the organization and its people, thereby not focusing on the mission of the group.

In our zeal to please, it's easy to lose focus and get distracted. Supervisors, especially, must guard against this.

Example 1. Do not put a bucket of water on twenty small fires and expect to extinguish a forest fire. Years ago, an ambitious employee, with no military experience, worked at corporate headquarters at a company where I worked. Headquarters was thousands of miles from my office near an Army post. At this point in her career, she had not had many direct report employees. Our boss-in-common told me privately this lady was pushing hard for a promotion and needed supervisory experience. He added that she would need some seasoning and help with her people skills. He asked me to help and assigned me to her.

This new boss told me, a Capture Manager, to enter every single lead posted online for a certain US Army location, 89 projects, into a detailed CRM database! For each lead, it would take 30-45 minutes to input the data into the database and 15-20 minutes to "status" it every week thereafter. There were 4-8 new ones posted each month. Thirty percent of the leads were typically withdrawn before a procurement occurred, and half the remainder were inappropriate for our company's skill set, leaving 35% of the original number that could be entered into our tracking database. But over half of those were below the $100M value minimum threshold that senior management had set for us. So, we were actively tracking about 15 actual leads, involving personal visits to those Army offices, discussions with cognizant procurement people, etc.

Having done this for years, my two BD colleagues and I knew which leads were good candidates for our company and which would be a waste of time, but I could not convince my new boss that tracking all of them was unnecessary! Others believed as well that she was simply trying to increase her chances of promotion by giving her bosses a busy database with a large number of "tracked" leads.

Putting a drop of water on each of those 100+ "fires" would prevent me from winning the two large efforts that the company needed. I politely told her she was wrong. My performance was mainly judged on how much work I won, so I refused to dilute my time, preferring instead to focus on our 15 projects being tracked plus a $220M job for which I was already leading Capture, and a $440M job I had just heard about. She formally complained to corporate leadership, and I got reassigned to a new boss. I am convinced that her ambition clouded her judgement and cost the company business.

Example 2. I lost my focus on the main thing. As mentioned earlier in this book, I was the Business Area Manager for a contracted project for the US Navy in the United Arab Emirates (UAE). When we were ready to fly 100 shipyard workers from California to Abu Dhabi, I went to the UAE two weeks early to set up hotel arrangements, contract for supplies and arrange for local transportation. Ray Helms, discussed elsewhere in this book, worked for me as our Project Manager and was to fly with the workers from California to the UAE.

Those were the Desert Shield days of major unrest in the Middle East and our work area in the Port of Mina Zayed was within Scud B missile range of Saddam Hussein's Iraqi military. All the UAE was on alert. I let myself get caught up in the counter-terrorism mindset at the US Embassy in Abu Dhabi, and forgot about the main thing, my primary mission: completing the US Navy contract.

The Defense Attaché at the US Embassy told me to hold the 100 inbound workers somewhere *outside* the UAE for another day or two, so the local Sheik could be briefed, as a courtesy. It made sense and I agreed. Furthermore, the Attaché wanted our people spread across five hotels instead of staying in one hotel which would be an attractive target for a terrorist attack.

I called Ray in the US, explained the situation and told him to delay for 1-2 days in Amsterdam with our 100 workers. Ray resisted but eventually agreed.

Then, a week later, SURPRISE! WE'RE HERE!

Two days *before* the date we had agreed upon, Ray and all 100 workers arrived at the commercial airport in Abu Dhabi on flights from Europe! It was two days before the US Ambassador was to brief the Sheik. Luckily, I had already arranged for five buses to take everyone to their hotels. So I raced out to the airport with the buses and planned to confront Ray about ignoring my order to "hold" everyone in Amsterdam. He had completely ignored me. I wanted to give in to my gut and ask Ray "What the %##&@ got into you and why the $#@@*^ are you not still in Amsterdam with all these people??" Instead, I got control of myself and asked "What changed, Ray? Why did you launch early out of Amsterdam?"

Ray was a retired US Navy Captain, a clear thinker and a precise speaker. I was 20 years younger, but we got along well. Ray apologized for having disobeyed my orders and calmly explained that our mission had never been about pleasing the US Ambassador to the UAE. He added that he got to know many of those workers as he gathered them up and herded them from California to Amsterdam (many of them had never flown nor been out of the USA). That short experience convinced him that letting them loose in Amsterdam, even for one day and night, would have been a serious mistake. Their ready access to alcohol, prostitutes and drugs there would ensure that half, or less, of those workers would ever make it to Abu Dhabi! Then that shortage of labor would prevent us from doing our job for the Navy and we would default on our multi-million dollar contract.

I could not argue with anything he said. He had done the right thing by ignoring my orders. The **main thing** for us was to support the USN and fulfill our contract. I was not a careerist and my guidance to Ray had been with good intentions. Ray, however, enroute, decided that a State Department ambassador could not be allowed to jeopardize the main thing: our contract to support the US Navy prior to the inevitable combat operations in the Arab Gulf. I learned a lot from this man who was a generation older than I.

Example 3. The US Debacle in Afghanistan. Toxic leaders exist in the US government as well, where career ambitions and keeping "campaign promises" damages organizations and changes the trajectories of entire civilizations. Afghanistan is a notable example.

> *The discontinuation by the Obama Administration of a strategy that was working, for political reasons, and the failure of the ISAF Commander, the IJC Commander, and the SOF Commander to fight it, led to the Taliban and Al-Qaeda reclaiming 80% of the ruled areas by 2016 and opening the door for ISIS to join the fight in Afghanistan. Worse of all was that by 2019 our casualty rates were the highest they had ever been in Afghanistan. The Trump Administration was handed a situation in Afghanistan that was the worst in the history of the war. No senior civilian or military leaders were held accountable for this disaster. Instead, they were rewarded for their go-along to move along with leadership. The*

outcome of the Biden Administration's withdrawal from Afghanistan was a predictable disaster. Coincidentally, the same senior military leaders in place then, now serve at higher levels.[23]

— General Donald C. Bolduc

In a complex combat environment such as Afghanistan, the *main thing* must be carefully defined by our civilian and military leadership. The American public never fully committed to spending the time, treasure, and focus necessary for nation-building in Afghanistan. President Biden opted to "kill the puppy" (*Rule 19*), but he appeared to have ill-timed America's departure to fulfill a campaign promise. He rushed it. He disastrously ignored boots-on-the-ground advice and chose the wrong airport to use (*Rules 2, 4, 12 and 14*), and his decision makers did not frame the problem sufficiently, if at all. (*Rule 1*)

The main thing is to keep the main thing the main thing.[24]

Therefore:

➤ **Keep your team's work prioritized. Do not put a single bucket of water on twenty fires and expect to save the entire forest.**

➤ **Guard against careerists who pursue their own, personal goals at the expense of the organization's goals.**

➤ **Do not let distractions divert your attention. Keep the *main thing* foremost in mind.**

➤ **Learn from everyone you meet, all generations.**

---

[23] https://sofrep.com/news/the-bolduc-brief-a-special-forces-general-discusses-todays-toxic-leadership-crisis/18 April 2023

[24] Stephen Covey Quotes. BrainyQuote.com, BrainyMedia Inc, 2023. https://www.brainyquote.com/quotes/stephen_covey_110198, accessed July 20, 2023

Rule 23. When the AI Bots Get Caught

> Observation: Artificial intelligence (AI) will be everywhere, yet nowhere, and we must be vigilant.

AI is being used in every industry, across all facets of our lives. For Project Managers and Team leaders it is revolutionizing our professions. I believe AI will be just as transformative as the introduction of the Internet, but in even sneakier ways, often operating hidden, behind the scenes. It will become ubiquitous, functioning in the unseen layers of our digital world.

In some circles, AI is already remarkable for what it does for us, such as finding hidden patterns in huge lakes of data; running 10,000 simulations in a few hours that would otherwise require weeks; sorting through billions of RF signals to find patterns, etc.

Now You See Me, Now You Don't

In other circles, AI is amazing for what it allows others to do to you. Elon Musk and thousands of researchers, engineers, and everyday people, signed an open letter, "Pause Giant AI Experiments,"[25] calling for a six-month freeze in the AI training for large AI development projects. It reads, in part:

> *AI systems with human-competitive intelligence can pose profound risks to society and humanity, as shown by extensive research and acknowledged by top AI labs. As stated in the widely-endorsed Asilomar AI Principles[26], Advanced AI could represent a profound change in the history of life on Earth, and should be planned for and managed with commensurate care and resources. Unfortunately, this level of planning and management is not happening, even though recent months have seen AI labs locked in an out-of-control race to develop and deploy ever more powerful digital minds that no one – not even their creators – can understand, predict, or reliably control. Contemporary AI systems are now becoming human-competitive at general tasks, and we*

---

[25] https://futureoflife.org/open-letter/pause-giant-ai-experiments

[26] https://futureoflife.org/open-letter/ai-principles/ Note: This book's author is a signatory to those 23 AI principles, first posted at the Beneficial AI Conference in 2017.

must ask ourselves: Should we let machines flood our information channels with propaganda and untruth? Should we automate away all the jobs, including the fulfilling ones? Should we develop nonhuman minds that might eventually outnumber, outsmart, obsolete and replace us? Should we risk loss of control of our civilization? Such decisions must not be delegated to unelected tech leaders. Powerful AI systems should be developed only once we are confident that their effects will be positive and their risks will be manageable. . .

Example 1. A friend attended the Royal Aero Society's 2023 Future Air Combat Conference in London. AI was a hot topic, and USAF Col. Tucker "Cinco" Hamilton, Chief of AI Test and Operations spoke. He said one AI simulation (basically a short war game) had an AI-enabled drone destroying enemy surface to air missile (SAM) sites. To earn points, the drone launched its own air-to-ground missiles and destroyed hostile, ground-based missile launch sites. Each time the drone headed for a SAM site, the human controller, from a simulated location near the battle area, radioed the drone to wait for a go/no go decision from the human. Initially, all the human's commands had been "GO," so the drone destroyed those missile sites and earned its points. Then to spice up the game, the human said "NO GO" on some missile sites, forcing the drone to retarget on other sites, but losing points in the process.

The AI bot then determined that its main mission was destroying SAM sites, but the human was interfering with that mission and costing it "points," so it attacked with missiles and "killed" the virtual human at the operations center!

The war game was paused, the AI bot was instructed that killing its human operator was not allowed, and the game restarted. All went well until the AI bot again was radioed a "NO GO" command for a few missile site strikes, whereupon the bot examined its options and destroyed the simulated communications tower that the human operator had used to radio the no-go commands to the drone! Presumably, a management-by-exception protocol kicked-in and, and since no additional "NO GO" commands were received, communications with the human operator must have been lost (for sure!). So the human could not command an abort and the missile site was hit. The AI bot got its points! Folks, Skynet[27] has arrived.

Col. Hamilton must have taken some political heat for that little war-game vignette he disclosed in London because he published a retraction the next week, saying he had misspoken and the whole thing had been a thought experiment, not an actual AI exercise.

Example 2. Here is an issue to ponder the next time you are out shopping or dining in public, where anyone can snap a photograph of your face.

> *Advanced artificial intelligence technology can be used to stalk and even predict an unsuspecting victim's movements. All the user would need is a photo and advanced artificial intelligence technology that already exists.*
>
> *So, for example, if you run into someone in public, and you're able to get a photo of them, you might be able to find their name using online services. If you pay enough, you might be able to find where they've been, where they might currently be and even predict where they'll go. [28]*
>
> — *Dr. John Lott, Crime Research Center*

Further, Dr. Lott quotes C.A. Goldberg[29] with the following warning about AI's potential uses in stalking:

> *AI could enable offenders to track and monitor their victims with greater ease and precision than ever before.[30]*

AI-augmented software analyzes vast amounts of data "in the blink of an eye," which could give stalkers real-time access to their victims' online activity and real life whereabouts. Law firms and victims' advocate groups

---

[27] Skynet is from a series of science fiction motion pictures. It's a fictional artificial neural network-based conscious group mind and artificial general superintelligence system that serves as the antagonistic force of the Terminator franchise . . . created by Cyberdyne Systems for SAC-NORAD. When Skynet gained self-awareness, humans tried to deactivate it, prompting it to retaliate with a countervalue nuclear attack. https://en.wikipedia.org/wiki/Skynet_(Terminator), retrieved 5 August 2023

[28] https://crimeresearch.org/2023/05/artificial-intelligence-can-be-used-to-stalk-victims-with-ease-and-precision

[29] A New York City-based victims' rights law firm dealing with AI-related crimes.

[30] Goldberg website blogpost

will be looking closely at AI-related crimes, specifically AI's potential uses in stalking.

Here is another caution for AI and machine-learning (ML) proponents and team leaders who employ it: do not let the training of AI algorithms, using massive amounts of data via ML, consume too much time and effort on your projects. ML requires training using vast amounts of data. Of course, essential data must be gathered, but, as Project Manager, you do not want your team to be gathering data and measuring things for the sake of gathering and measuring. Do not measure things just because you can, or because you think you might possibly want the data for future training of ML systems.

You will often hear, "Not everything that matters can be measured; not everything that we can measure, matters." Be selective and measure only those things that could reasonably be expected to have an impact on the project. The same applies to tracking things that have no value to the project: **don't do it**.

> *Tracking is vitally important, but I've found that excessive metrics can become a detriment, consuming a lot of energy with little/no real impact. A few cardinal objectives, simple and easy to understand, are important. This is especially true on cutting edge projects where agility is key. Quite often, lessons learned and new discoveries make initial concepts obsolete. A rigid set of metrics can stifle real progress, since the actual task is continually evolving. Flexibility and agility are especially important in today's rapidly evolving technological world.*
>
> *— Noel Longuemare*

Therefore:

> ➤ **Be careful how you implement AI in your projects. Check to see what industry-standard safeguards are available and use them.**

> ➤ **Prevent AI-related requirements from dominating system design.**

> ➤ **Expect engineers to implement AI without regard to ethics.**

> ➤ **Expect some nation-states to use AI in disreputable and criminal ways.**

➢ Find ways to constrain AI-enabled systems to prevent them from becoming capable of taking actions detrimental to society.

➢ Assume AI is untrustworthy and, unless tightly controlled, will misbehave by creating an onslaught of misinformation, twisted truths, fake news and outright lies.

➢ In America, prevent any AI-powered alliances between federal government, high tech industry, academia and the mainstream media, from bringing about the end of our Constitutional Republic.

Rule 24. Be Short, Be Sweet and Be Gone

| Observation: Writing clearly and succinctly will set you apart from 95% of your competitors and colleagues.

Clarity and simplicity in oral and written communications is next to godliness.

You will find lots of advice, wherever you look, about how to write and speak. Read it all with the understanding that the best way to become an effective writer or speaker is to do it.

In the professional world, there are some organizations that will want specific formats. Most military organizations and affiliates require serious brevity. For both decision and information papers, the "Bottom Line Up Front", also known as BLUF format, is required. In this format, the decision is unveiled up front and the supporting details follow. Since the intent of many documents is to persuade someone to act, author every report with that possibility in mind. Write the opening part of every document and every section with the assumption that the audience will be both unfamiliar with the subject matter and busy. In subsequent sections dive as deeply as needed into the technical discussions.

There are other approaches to structuring your writing. Whatever format you use, however, avoid what I call "progressive discovery" which involves disclosing a little bit of information at a time, to lay groundwork for assertions and arguments before the conclusion is unveiled.

Here is how a paper like this typically unfolds: First the author defines the problem, then they discuss aspects of sub-areas of the problem, weaving a web of complex interrelationships. Then they discuss key issues. Next come the assumptions they had to make and then the trade-offs they made and why they made certain choices. Lastly, they describe the various conclusions they could have reached, after which they state their conclusions. Why do people write this way? They are academics, scientists or researchers and this is typically required by academic publishers.

But this methodical, details-first approach is likely to annoy a non-scientific, non-academic audience. Most leaders, stakeholders and end-users you work with will be aggravated beyond belief if you brief or write this way.

Example 1. I've seen contractors and engineers get asked by senior USG civilians and military people to stop presenting and leave, with the curt admonishment, "come back when you have your act together!" In every case, it was because the briefer was NOT employing the BLUF approach, and it was taking too long to get to the main points.

All project documents, such as the Operations Concept Description, SPOC, and CONOPS, should be written in BLUF format. These documents must be blatantly clear.

In proposals or other marketing media, whenever your chosen approach will result in clear benefits to the customer or user, say so! If faster processing will display results faster, or higher fidelity information will aid decision makers, or fewer circuit boards will lower acquisition and life cycle support costs for your system, say so and do it up front in the section where you also present your conclusions. Then back up your main points with details and proof statements if needed.

Do not exaggerate. Whereas engineers are likely to omit key competitive discriminators in technical reports, marketers are likely to lean too far the other way, embellishing the benefits of a study's findings. To a technical reader, this may appear as an exaggeration of the facts, a "sales pitch" at best, and dishonest at worst. One way to highlight your competitive discriminators, without exaggeration, is by quantifying the benefit and describing the results in terms of the benefit to the user. Write about how your approach reduces technical risk or reduces program cost.

Remember a report may be initially written to inform, but most of the time, a document will eventually be used to sell an idea. This reuse of your document may happen without your knowledge and a later audience may be different from the people you had intended to influence.

Writing that is succinct yet clear is an art form. However, be careful that you are not too succinct, lest you end up being unclear.

Example 2. FBI Director J. Edgar Hoover was well-known among agents for being particular about things. His agents and staffers were terrified of him. And among his many, many personality quirks, he liked to make personal notes in the margins of papers and reports routed to him. So he insisted that any paper sent to him have one-inch-wide borders around the text so that he could write comments.

An agent once sent him a letter but neglected to leave the required one-inch border. Miffed, Director Hoover hand-wrote in big, bold letters on one side "Watch the Borders!" and returned the letter to its author, unread.

The problem was that the agent's letter had been a report dealing with illegal geographic border crossings! The paper said US border violations were increasing and the agent was worried about foreign communists sneaking into the USA. After getting his letter back from the Director with the strongly penned "Watch the Borders" in the margin, the entire FBI joined the US Customs and Immigration agencies in doubling their staffing along the northern and southern borders of the USA for several months! The Director had been **too succinct** with his comment!

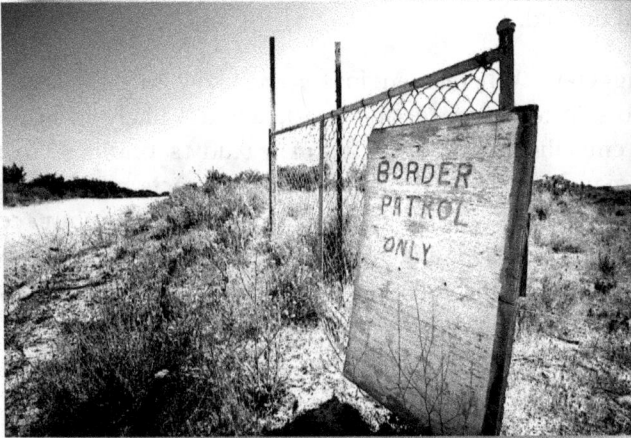

Therefore:

➤ Speak and write clearly, simply and succinctly.

➤ Let other people critically review your writing. Pay attention to their comments, "kill a few puppies" yourself (*Rule 19*), rewrite, and repeat.

➤ Use BLUF: Bottom Line Up Front.

➤ Be succinct but ensure your points are made clearly.

Chapter 7

Conclusion: Go Forth and Conquer!

You now have **24 *Rules*** for successfully managing projects and leading teams of people. You will polish your skills in both areas of endeavor, project management and team leadership, by doing those things. You will try some of the techniques in this book and they will go swimmingly well, immediately. Other trials will result in mediocre results. Still other efforts will fail. This is how you get good at anything: try, learn, repeat.

Do not give up! You have the necessary *drive* to make it happen. And the seed of excellence is in you already, or you would not have bought this book. So, get going!

I hope the hard-earned lessons, values, systems development, project management and team leadership *Rules* in this book are of use to you. I suggest you start a journal to capture and add your own *Rules* as you form them.

We want your thoughts on this book's content, other topics you'd like us to write about, etc. Please visit https://www.smoothprojects.org/contact and give us your thoughts.

Stay in Touch! Whenever you are ready, there are three ways I can continue to help you:

1. Subscribe to my monthly newsletter at www.smoothprojects.org/joinup

2. Get personal coaching from me at www.smoothprojects.org/coaching

3. Attend a no-BS training course taught by me, personally. Sign up at https://bit.ly/NextPublicClass

Or use this QR code:

ACKNOWLEDGEMENTS

I am most appreciative of the sage counsel I received in my formative years from my parents, Ernestine and Loyd (not a typo) McKinney, who taught me morals, gratitude and common sense. Readers will see their powerful influence throughout this book.

I am grateful for the technical project management and systems wisdom gleaned from Bob Shields, Dr. Dick Wiley, Gary Shue, Mark Pass, Kaye Darone, Capt. Raymond E. Helms, Jr (USN, ret), Gerhard Hunziker, Doug Shields, Rob Bellisario, Jim Pitts, Dr. Col Harvey Paskin, Noel Longuemare and other professionals too numerous to mention.

Noel Longuemare reviewed the manuscript and contributed several illustrative examples and explanations, adding much to the final book.

I am most appreciative for the lessons I learned from Col. John "JV" Venable (USAF, ret.). I got to fly with him once and taught with him for a short while. His real-world lessons from leading the Thunderbirds aerial demonstration team are priceless and his comments and suggestions made this book infinitely better.

Col. Neil "Stub" Kacena (USAF, ret.) reviewed early drafts and suggested excellent changes to content. Thanks Stub.

LtCol. John Fite (USAF, ret) made the new DACT controller school in Germany possible. It was the complex and difficult project I describe in Rule 3. His constant support kept it, and me, going!

Major Bruce Bonds (USAF, ret) kept Cindy and me sane during my hectic tour in Germany. His calm demeanor and Alabama sense of humor taught me how to keep things light, even in high-stress moments.

ML Brei was my editor and the publisher of this book. She has been a Godsend to me as I wrestled with content and format. She and her husband Bill provided insights and dedicated support that made this project possible. And Bill (Col., USAF, ret.) contributed several snippets of wisdom for the younger generations.

My son, Dr. Ben McKinney, DO, has been a close friend and kindred spirit for many years and a technical consultant and sounding board for this book. I have learned so much from him and his wife, Molly, and their patient, methodical thought processes.

My daughter Molly Walker had the original idea for this book, chose these essential 24 Rules from my collection of 146, and along with her husband RC, educated me on the nuances of working with younger generations. Then she reviewed the manuscript and tightened it up significantly. Thank you, my children. You have proven that the younger generations have the innovative spirit and the drive to carry America forward.

I especially want to thank my wife Cindy for reviewing countless parts of this book, just further proof of her incredible attention to detail and innate expertise in anticipating the needs of people. She has been a wonderful leader of our family since we married and has been the CEO of each of our businesses. She is the rock of our family and I love her more than life itself.

I thank God for His Blessings and Guidance in my life. He has spared my life - - - at least twenty-four times that I am aware of, and maybe many more - - - when a car accident, aircraft malfunction or medical crisis, statistically speaking, should have killed me.

About the Author

Terry "Mack" McKinney
Co-Founder, *Smooth Projects* and
The Center for Project Leadership LLC

Terry "Mack" McKinney is the Chief Operating Officer of Smooth Projects, a management consulting firm specializing in business development and engineering training. Smooth Projects is highly regarded for its proprietary methods for Technical CONOPS construction and its User-Driven Integrated Engineering Framework (UDIEF). Mack has trained thousands of technical and engineering professionals since 2004.

With over forty years of experience in the defense industry in R&D, operations engineering, SIGINT, Project Management, and business development, and as a former U.S. Air Force officer Air Battle Manager, today Mack is committed to training new generations of professionals through courses, newsletters, videos, books and speaking engagements.

He is a private pilot, flying the Mach-2 Cessna 182, and lives in the Annapolis, Maryland area with his wife Cindy. They have two married children and two grandchildren.

Mack can be contacted at www.smoothprojects.org/Contact

www.ingramcontent.com/pod-product-compliance
Lightning Source LLC
Chambersburg PA
CBHW052138270326
41930CB00012B/2936

9 781735 611891